Endless Possibilities

Dear Chet,
Thanks for providing me with so many endless possibilities at Haynes.
Love,
Judy

P.S. Don't forget Chapter #4 to read

Endless Possibilities

Generating Curriculum in Social Studies and Literacy

Edited by Pat Cordeiro

with
Judy Blatt, Bill Brummett, Carli Carrara,
Bobbi Fisher, Lisa Burley Maras, Jane Rowe,
Linda Squire, and Sandra Wilensky

HEINEMANN
Portsmouth, NH

HEINEMANN
A division of Reed Elsevier Inc.
361 Hanover Street
Portsmouth, NH 03801-3912

Offices and agents throughout the world

The authors wish to thank those who granted permission to reprint previously published material:

> Page 94: Figure 6–1. Adapted by permission of Kathy G. Short and Carolyn Burke: *Creating Curriculum: Teachers and Students as a Community of Learners* (Heinemann, A division of Reed Elsevier Inc., Portsmouth, NH, 1991).

Every effort has been made to contact the copyright holders and students for permission to reprint borrowed material. We regret any oversights that may have occurred and would be happy to rectify them in future printings of this work.

Library of Congress Cataloging-in-Publication Data

Endless possibilities : generating curriculum in social studies and
    literacy / edited by Pat Cordeiro, with Judy Blatt . . . [et al.].
        p.   cm.
    Includes bibliographical references.
    ISBN 0-435-08903-X
    1. Social sciences—Study and teaching (Elementary)—United
States—Curricula.   2. Language arts (Elementary)—United States—
Curricula.   3. Interdisciplinary approach in education—United
States.   4. Curriculum planning—United States.   I. Cordeiro, Pat,
1944–   .
LB1584.E46   1995
372.83043—dc20   94–48367
                                                       CIP

Acquisitions Editor: Carolyn Coman
Production Editor: Renée M. Pinard
Cover Designer: Darci Mehall

Printed in the United States of America on acid-free paper
99 98 97 96 95 EB 1 2 3 4 5 6

....

This book is dedicated by the editor—

to my mother, Elizabeth Locke,
who, through her life, her teaching, her painting, and her writing,
brings social studies to life.

Contents

Acknowledgments

My thanks to the teachers who have contributed to this volume. Their patience, hard work, and dedication to learning and teaching have gone beyond the bounds of simple authorship. Together we recognize that those of us collected here represent a small portion of the fine work in social studies, literacy, and whole language that is going on behind closed school doors across the country. I wish all teachers the chance to share their programs with other teachers as we have done here, and I hope this book will inspire others to talk and write about the innovations and inspirations they and their students are enjoying.

I'm grateful to those who provided feedback on the early versions of this text: the reviewers selected by the Heinemann editors; my friends Dr. Pat Lyons and Professor Nikki Thomas, both of Rhode Island College; and Dina Sechio, sixth-grade teacher extraordinaire. Many others—teachers I have met across the country and colleagues back home at Rhode Island College—have offered support and encouragement, and I thank them all. Thanks also to the teacher I met at the 1994 Whole Language Umbrella conference in San Diego who suggested that a similar volume in science should be the next step—I'll begin to think about that now.

I am very grateful for the support, encouragement, and sound advice of my editor at Heinemann, Carolyn Coman, whose good wishes and insightful suggestions sustained me, and to Renée Pinard, whose copyediting help was invaluable. Thanks also to all at Heinemann who have worked to make this volume the very best production it could be.

I am, as ever, grateful to my friend Bobbi Fisher for her ongoing talk and support. The company of like minds makes all the difference. And I am grateful to my friend Philippa Stratton for her support when this book was just an idea in my mind.

I thank my mother, Betty Locke, for her midnight talks about the world of social studies and literacy and for her readings and response to early drafts. Thanks to my sister, Sandy May, whose questioning mind and background in history help so much. And closest to home,

I am blessed with the support of my husband, Marty, for his unfailing patience and encouragement and for keeping the home fires burning. Thanks to you all for helping me out once again.

PAT CORDEIRO

Preface

When I enter Carli Carrara's classroom, I'm in a rainforest. Children sit reading beneath the trees, animals appear to come and go through the foliage. It's an overwhelming impression. Stretching across the floor, up the chalkboard, and over the classroom ceiling, the trees built by Carli and the boys and girls are huge and lush and dominate the surroundings. To a learner's fertile imagination—mine included—it's a small step to walk across this classroom and into a rainforest as real as any in the world, to dwell in a world transcending the classroom.

Over my years of teaching, I have been continually impressed with the wonderful things going on in classrooms. Teachers and their students are building classroom cities, creating environments, traveling imaginary oceans, designing future technology, and all within closed doors. Many of the fine and innovative programs—schools' best ideas—are never known by others.

Perhaps closed doors are a prerequisite for the kind of growth we see in innovative classrooms. Classrooms are in their way greenhouses—closed, self-contained environments with all the necessities for great and grand growth. Comparing successful classrooms to flourishing greenhouses, we find similar components: rich and fertile soil in the imaginations, energy, and enthusiasm of the teachers and boys and girls; rare and exotic plants in the way of projects and interests that people are excited about growing and tending; food and water in the way of classroom interaction, emergent research, and feedback and interest from friends; and a productive and fertile environment in the way of rich classroom communities and a climate conducive to collaborative learning and teaching.

But greenhouses need ventilation, too, and ventilation comes to the classroom through the seeking of ideas and resources by the teacher and by the children. In this book, we hope to bring some new thoughts and innovations to readers. I've asked eight teachers I know to take us into their "greenhouses," to describe the projects they and their students do as they integrate three compatible aspects of curriculum: social studies, literacy, and whole language. These three elements of what we teach are particularly suited for each other and have served to centralize the life of the classroom in many settings. In the Introduction, we will look at these three areas and consider why they are so complementary.

In the classrooms we visit here, the integration of these particular subject areas comes about through a process of growth we call "a generative curriculum." This designation came originally from Don Holdaway one morning over breakfast as he, Bobbi Fisher, and I explored aspects of the entity we call "curriculum." Don used the term *generative* in company with the idea of developmental curriculum, one that reflects the developmental strengths of the learners it affects. Such a curriculum would be markedly different in goals and structure from one that is a "trickle-down" from a college curriculum, a miniaturization of a curriculum appropriate for much older learners.

The idea of developmentally appropriate curriculum continues to influence our thinking, but the term *generative curriculum* has come to mean a great deal more to those of use who find it the best description for what we do. In Chapter 1, we will explore more fully this idea of what it means to generate a curriculum and how that is an influence on the chapters that follow.

The teachers profiled here have undergone a process of evolution and development themselves. Each of their accounts of classroom life, practice, and curriculum is preceded by a section called "About —." These sections usually originated in an interview with the chapter author, and the written version was often a collaboration between the author and me. Each classroom account includes a section on assessment written by the author and is followed by a section entitled "Pat Reflects," in which I relate sections to each other and to the themes of the book.

One of the greatest influences on my own teaching has been the personal narrative of teachers who have sought change and are in the midst of accomplishing it. As they talk about how they came to where they are now, I see myself as a teacher in a state of change, and I see the possibilities for future direction.

In Chapter 2, Bobbi Fisher explores a new phenomenon, first graders who saw themselves as a community of informed learners in a sophisticated and abstract activity, note taking. In Chapter 3, Sandra Wilensky demonstrates the innovations possible in generating a curriculum with second graders who were readers and writers of social studies. In Chapter 4, Judy Blatt traces the path of her generative use of three forms of simulations to inspire her own and her third-grade students' learning. Chapter 5 is Carli Carrara's reflection on her rain forest unit and her thoughts on how curriculum in her room is changing and growing, being generated and created. Chapter 6 is written by a team of teachers, Lisa Maras and Bill Brummett. In it they explore how team teaching in a multi-age classroom, grades three and four together, allowed them to follow students' lead, learning from the students what needed to be learned about understanding the American electoral process. In Chapter 7, Linda Squire, a music teacher, shows how she melded and integrated her own curriculum with the social studies and literacy curricula of the school. In Chapter 8, Jane Rowe discusses successes and problems she encountered as she integrated a classroom economic system into the school social studies curriculum incorporating innovations generated by her students.

The Epilogue to this book discusses learning and adaptability: How can teachers from other grades and teachers in other settings adapt, stretch, and evaluate the ideas from these teachers? What are some of the mechanisms that made these programs work? How can a generative curriculum help?

One of the main mechanisms for this kind of fertile change is the sharing of ideas between teachers. Very often we can envision and construct programs together that otherwise might seem overwhelming when considered in solitude. Part of the success of these programs comes from the view these special teachers have of themselves as learners first, teachers second, and from the sharing they do with other teachers. They see a generative curriculum as a support system for change and integration in classroom life.

The chapters in this book are not displays in a museum. Or, to continue the greenhouse metaphor, the situations discussed here are not rare and exotic plants that only experts can grow. They are living, organic processes, meant to be shaped and molded, handled and activated. They flourish in many settings because the climate is right and the conditions appropriate. Sometimes they spring up in classrooms as suddenly as wildflowers in a field, and sometimes teachers and children seek them out like rare plants, importing them from other settings. We hope that teachers across the grades will read this book across the chapters, and, seeing possibilities in each account, will find themselves saying, "I could do that . . ."

The Triad: Social Studies, Literacy, and Whole Language

Pat Cordeiro

Social Studies as Reading

I remember my early days of teaching social studies. They were a lot like my old school days of learning social studies. We got out the books, and we read. As a teacher, I justified this to myself on the basis of standardized tests—if we didn't learn to read all that hard stuff in the classroom, all together, come what may, how would we ever be able to do it alone on standardized tests? Thus one fed the other. The daily reading fed the testing, and the testing fed the ritual reading.

My trouble as a teacher with this ritual reading was—the students in my class. One-third loved it, or at least they appeared to love it. They read, they didn't lose their places, they answered my questions (such as those questions were), they seemed to be paying attention. But the other two-thirds—they were all over the map. There were those few who I knew were completely lost, gone-out-the-window, not getting anything out of this. There were a few who needed to be perpetually "sat on," who I had to keep after just to get them to be quiet so that we could do what I thought we were supposed to be doing. And then there were a whole lot who just didn't seem to be getting anything out of anything—especially in social studies. They didn't answer the questions, they usually didn't even put their hands up. The same kids always put their hands up. I took it as my great failing as a teacher that I wasn't able to devise an interesting way to hear everything from everybody all the time, that I couldn't get everyone to respond. I thought there was something wrong with me.

Today when I ask my college students to respond to their memories of social studies, it seems to me that almost all of them were in this category—those who were getting nothing out of what was happening, those for whom social studies was always a dead subject, something for hot Friday afternoons, something for somebody else to respond to and

1

for everybody else to lie low during. And sometimes they do blame it on their teachers—those teachers who also appeared to hate social studies, who saw no joy in exploring the life of the world and humankind. And I understand: we were all limited by the limits of our teachers.

I might be able to salvage some good from these memories if I could see those old activities somehow as an integration of social studies and literacy, a blending of reading, writing, and social studying. But it wasn't. This was social studies mapped directly onto literacy, or perhaps the other way around, with literacy using social studies as a mere vehicle. Either way, this was a direct stamping of the two, with both literacy and social studies coming up short. Literacy came up short because this was not real reading. If this kind of round-robin reading had any effect on our literacy, it was to leave us with the sour aftertaste or dreaded fear of mandated performance of reading of difficult material and the sworn commitment to never, never read such stuff again, especially aloud.

It seems to me that social studies loses out altogether in our old round-robin reading. Almost without exception, I find that adults report that social studies as a subject area has no meaning for them, if they can relate to it at all. A few don't even remember what it was supposed to be. Those who can recall an apparent purpose in what they were doing talk about reading and not about social studies. Few relate social studies to the world around them.

One of the worst aspects of this social-studies-as-reading-aloud was that a vibrant, essential, and multifaceted subject area became a reading test. For those of us who were good readers, we had the fun of enacting a piece of the round-robin puzzle, counting ahead to find and mentally rehearsing our paragraphs, and idly trailing along with the halting reading performances of our less confident, sweating comrades. Those who were poor or unsure readers now report counting ahead with trepidation, studying the words silently, hoping that they hadn't counted the paragraphs wrong, praying that they wouldn't get called on to answer a question they didn't hear while they were practicing, knowing that soon they would have to perform.

A significant content-area aspect of that attitude was that none of us really had any time to pay attention to the substance of what other readers were reading. We only focused on our own paragraph of social studies, and then only for reading aloud—performing—the words. And, to make things worse, there were the teachers who called on readers randomly. When that happened, the class really focused on the word reading and not on the meaning behind the words.

I think that in spite of a teacher's best efforts to make social-studies-as-reading-aloud inviting and stimulating, its true life as a reading activity can never change. And as long as social studies is viewed by teachers and children as another way to test children's reading, social studies—a form of the social sciences—will never be the vibrant, living subject it can be for everyone.

Integrating Social Studies and Literacy Meaningfully

The kind of integration we are envisioning here is the kind expressed in Donald Graves's (1989) book *Investigate Nonfiction*. In that book, Don traces the uses of nonfiction reading and writing developmentally as they lead to deeper understanding of content and its expression. Don interweaves reading, writing, speaking, and listening throughout, without one becoming more important than another. For many of us, reading and writing became the sole means of expressing literacy, without regard for the other two essential elements, speaking and listening. Don keeps them all parallel.

In this framework of literacy, two kinds of classroom interactions become significant, the interpersonal interactions student-to-student and student-to-teacher, and the interaction between the four prongs of literacy—reading, writing, speaking, and listening. These form a matrix, providing opportunities for students to have the most important interaction of all—with the material to be learned. This is what Nancy Martin (1976) calls learning that is "felt on the pulses in order to be truly known" (33), an interaction with what is to be learned that allows children to actively engage in "establishing personal relevances in the information they have come across and relating new experience to their total picture of the world" (33).

By using reading as the sole mean of literate engagement with social studies, we place children in the position of being receivers of knowledge, rather than active users, creators, discoverers, and constructors of knowledge. My old teachers may well have felt that they were engaging me in learning social studies when they asked me to read round-robin. But in fact, I was only actively engaged during the time I had my turn. And then I was engaged in performing, not learning. When other kids were reading, I was thinking, or reading ahead, or daydreaming, or worse. I might even have slipped into some state of mind that leaves no trace. I don't remember fifth grade at all. Not at all. I can't even picture the teacher. Whatever must I have been doing during round-robin reading?

Even when teachers liven up round-robin reading with questions and answers, with coming up to the board and pointing to this and that, with references to pictures and charts, some students in the class do not need to attend. In even the smallest classrooms, most children can allow others to do the activity, usually simply by being quiet. Even those children who do get called on know that most of the time, when round-robin reading is the main mode of doing social studies, everyone will be pretty much left alone to drift, with only occasional teacherly interruptions.

Vital social studies requires active and ongoing engagement. My college students report good and strong memories from social studies about the projects they did. They remember meals they cooked and shared with parents, field trips they took, maps they built on plywood, plays they put on, programs they held. They report active and engaging interactions with each other and the material they were learning. They report movement and talk, using language to learn with and not as a mere decoding skill for hard material; they report remembering involvement with what Douglas Barnes (1976) calls "exploratory talk," literacy used to learn with, not to perform with.

Why Social Studies Leans on Interactive Learning

By its very nature, social studies depends on interactive processes. It draws concepts mainly from history and the disciplines of the social sciences. Social studies relies on linkages and connections. And today, social studies and social sciences place emphasis on making connections in a climate of critical thinking and reflection. The current goals of the National Commission on Social Studies in the Schools, published in their 1989 report "Charting a Course: Social Studies for the 21st Century," are fivefold and should enable students to develop:

1. Civic responsibility and active civic participation.
2. Perspectives on their own life experiences so they see themselves as part of the larger human adventure in time and place.
3. A critical understanding of the history, geography, economic, political and social institutions, traditions, and values of the United States as expressed in both their unity and diversity.
4. An understanding of other peoples and the unity and diversity of world history, geography, institutions, traditions and values.
5. Critical attitudes and analytical perspectives appropriate to analysis of the human condition. (6)

Goal one, civic responsibility and participation, was once the only goal of social studies, or so it seemed to me. We memorized presidents, memorized capitals, memorized the Preamble to the Constitution—or tried to—all in the name of civic responsibility. We pledged allegiance, analyzed the meaning of the pledge, sang patriotic songs every morning, read poems like "Paul Revere's Ride" and "Oh Captain, My Captain," and for some of us that was the extent of social studies.

But today, teachers are redesigning social studies understanding and going far beyond goal one, civic responsibility, and far beyond any text. In a pair of fifth-grade classrooms my college social studies methods class works with, we start from a mandated curriculum topic of American History. The focus in the fall is Native Peoples of North America, an approach to goal four, understanding other peoples. We begin from a conceptual base: *how* people live is directly related to *where* they live. This allows us to work with goal five, critical attitudes and perspectives. Out of our conceptual understanding springs the spontaneous insight that people live in different ways, and native people in past times also lived in different ways.

As we develop expert groups on tribes of native peoples from different regions of North America, we make use of goal three, critically understanding some of the disciplines and subject areas of social studies. We learn about geography—global, regional, and local—and connect that with the history of the tribes and bands we are studying; we discuss social institutions, such as family and government, and connect those topics to differing values and traditions; and we find that political and economic understandings become essential as we move toward the more modern history of the native peoples and consider their history of removals to reservations and their current ways of life. Students often spontaneously connect goal one, civic understandings, with goal five, as they critically assess the current life of tribes and how aspects of citizenship often taken for granted by others have affected native peoples. As our study moves outside of the realm of understanding of native peoples, we consider our own lives, over time through history and over space through geography—a direct result of goal two. We use our study of native peoples as a model for examining our own culture, connecting across all the goals and, particularly, to goal five.

Thus, the current goals of social studies lend themselves to ways of looking at the world, understanding our current and future condition, and seeing life through a social lens. As we go through this as teachers, we try to help students develop an understanding of how the various disciplines that make up social studies and the social sciences acquire and examine knowledge. So, while we look at the past of tribal groups, we try to think like historians. We ask ourselves, how would a historian search for this information? What do geographers do? In what ways could we do what an anthropologist does?

All of this work takes a lot of talk and understanding. Asking open-ended questions like those above requires that we give students time to use language productively, "as a means of learning" as Douglas Barnes puts it. And, to satisfy the five goals, we need projects and activities and big ideas, concepts in action. It is not possible to try to do all this through book reading. Goal five, in particular, requires that students think and reflect, read and write, speak and listen—in short, use literacy to its fullest, instead of in a rote fashion. Nancy Martin (1976) says, "It seems that information which is abstract and difficult to comprehend, or which touches on powerful themes and deep concerns, or which is in some idiosyncratic way personally relevant to the learner, involves the person more completely in coming to terms with it" (33). And that kind of coming to terms involves an interaction between literacy in its fullest definition combined with social studies in its most complete form. As Douglas Barnes says, "Whenever school learning has gone beyond meaningless rote, we can take it that a child has made some kind of relationship between what he knows already and what the school has presented" (22).

Situating a Curriculum in Whole Language

The blending of literacy and social studies is most successful when it happens in a hospitable climate such as that described by Brian Cambourne (1988) in his book *The Whole Story*. The kind of productive, exploratory talk, reading, and writing that leads to uses of all aspects of literacy and that fosters the development of deep conceptual understandings requires an environment which promotes interaction, trust, and dialogue. Such an environment is found in whole language classrooms. In *Joyful Learning: A Whole Language Kindergarten*, Bobbi Fisher (1991) says that there are three characteristics of such classrooms:

1. There is an abundance of print around the room.
2. Children . . . are involved in planning and managing their learning.
3. Children are trusted as the authorities of their own learning. (1)

In such settings, subject areas like social studies are blended and integrated and approached in a climate of *immersion*. Students are allowed to become engrossed in the material being explored, and they are allowed both time and space for learning. For example, if the specific topic being explored was the immigration to North America of the group we have come to call the Pilgrims, students would not just be asked to read material and to write a one-page diary entry as if they were a Pilgrim. Rather, students would be allowed to explore how it would feel to be in the Pilgrims' situation. They would be allowed "to walk in the time of the event" (Heathcote 1983, 695). Immersion in social studies means giving students and teacher the time and space to explore through research, projection, and pretending what it means to be someone else in another place.

In these classrooms, social studies and literacy are enhanced by teachers who are learners, too. Teachers in this triad of learning— literacy and social studies and whole language—are actively involved in the material, and they demonstrate a variety of things to the learners around them. First and foremost, they *demonstrate* themselves as learners, actively seeking and utilizing knowledge. Such teachers revel in new learning and tell their students about it, a far cry from my own past teachers who sent forth the message that they learned all there was to know before they ever met me. Whole language teachers demonstrate how they work with and integrate new knowledge; they model for young learners how to read, write, speak, and listen; and they tell young learners what they are doing and how they are doing it. They make their opaque processes of learning transparent. They show young learners how they teach and encourage young learners to teach, too. Whole language teachers believe the maxim that "we learn best by teaching," and they practice it in their classroom. By demonstrating teaching and learning processes to their students, teachers remove themselves from the role of content experts and become instead experts in the art of learning and teaching, eager and willing to share that knowledge. And so in a Pilgrim Immigration experience, the "teacher as learner" would become part of the learning journey, too, actively involved in the content learning taking place, actively demonstrating how teachers go about searching and exploring this topic, and modeling for students how teachers blend literacy and social studies.

In these classrooms, there is an *expectation* that everyone will learn and do well, that everyone—including the teacher—wants to be part of the learning process, that everyone thinks of themselves as members of what Frank Smith (1988) calls "the literacy club." I noticed this issue of expectation most clearly one year when I did demonstration lessons across my state in classrooms new to me. When I went into those classrooms with my writing-to-learn program, all students in the class participated equally. I asked them to write informally and then read aloud to the class a thought they had written that seemed to them to summarize "something everyone should know about the topic." Usually there were also special education students brought in for the demonstration time so their teachers could observe me. Not knowing who was who, I expected them all to do equally well, and my trust in their abilities was always rewarded. Expectation of success is a powerful thing and needs to be first and foremost.

In a climate of immersion, learners and teachers are all actively *engaged* in activities and exploration. Sometimes this seems hard to accomplish; not everything we have to learn is intrinsically engaging for all learners. Multiplication tables come to mind as an example, as does handwriting. In some cases, as with multiplication tables, game formats are used, whole or small group, so that learners are engaged by the nature of the activity rather than by the subject matter itself. In other cases, as with handwriting, teachers reassess the nature of the skill or material to be learned, weigh its value, and deliver it into the classroom in small doses, using engaging format to help make the subject matter engaging. In social studies, more and more teachers are lengthening the time of study for a subject so that students have time to get engaged. After all, teachers often spend the whole summer being engaged in a particular area that *they* wish to learn. And they draw students into activities that engage them in a social studies topic or concept by giving them the opportunity to explore and "try out" the life of the people involved through simulations and role-playing.

Particularly in the area of social studies, encouraging students to make *approximations* helps them to take risks and explore new territories. In doing an approximation, a learner studies a model or demonstration and then tries to re-create what is observed. Often the attempt is less than perfect, but it moves constantly toward the model. In social studies, students are encouraged to try out the role of a geographer, for instance, or to explore how a historian might learn about something new. In trying out these new roles, students—and teachers—need room to do the best they can, to experiment, to revise, to play with social studies. And in the process, they need to receive positive feedback from peers, teachers, and parents about how their approximations are doing. Thus, they move closer to the goal.

The feedback students receive for their attempts at new learning are the *response* of the classroom. By including response as one of the optimal conditions of learning, we give recognition to the absolute need for interaction, movement, and talk in this setting. For instance, as students explore through activities what life was like for the Pilgrims—

why they made the decisions they did, how their life evolved into our life—they share their learning. This sharing gives an opportunity for the growth of what Douglas Barnes calls "exploratory talk," the kind of talk between learners that demands response and reaction, that allows everyone in the classroom the chance to make the learning their own.

One of the major elements of these settings is the opportunity for *use*. In my old social studies learning days, we never had opportunities for use and were not expected to practice what we were learning. Rather, it was what my friend Linda Erdmann calls "sit and git"—a situation without active use. In fact, I would say that the only time we actually used any part of the social studies we were learning was when we went out onto the playground and were expected to put into operation all the noble things we had learned about citizenship, equality, and good government. It was hard, since we really grew up in an autocratic, teacher-led society, which told us about imaginary democratic societies without any opportunities for use.

Finally, these classrooms offer students the chance to take *responsibility* for their own learning. In doing this, students are helped to become good choice makers, good personal schedulers, good decision makers, and good problem solvers, through an active combination of all the other conditions that have gone before. Use gives students a chance to practice choice making and decision making, and as they observe demonstrations and try out their own in the form of approximations, students actively engage with the material, responding to each other. Teachers and students create a climate of immersion in the learning at hand, expecting that all will succeed. In my old social studies days, there was literally no element of responsibility, short of being sure to be prepared for the inevitable. We were told what to learn, and when and how to learn it. Whether or not the material seemed of value was something I think not even my teachers assessed.

Weaving Whole Language, Social Studies, and Literacy Together

In the profiles in this book, we can see the weaving together of these three elements. Literacy in all the grades is used as a tool for exploring the world around us. Reading, writing, speaking, and listening are *all* seen as ways of acquiring and developing new knowledge. At the intersection of the three themes are found common elements of social development and communication, critical thinking, active learning, and integration. In programs that weave a fabric of these elements, there is a flexibility and flow between them, so that philosophy of learning and teaching (whole language), content and values (social studies), and roles of learning and teaching about the world (literacy) become continuous and interdependent.

To me this goes beyond what is commonly called "integration." Many of us have spent much time trying to detect whether or not we were "doing integration," searching for subject areas that were compatible, designing worksheets that had numbers *and* print, bending our programs and ourselves to try to fit an amorphous model of "integration." To me, the weaving of a fabric of philosophy, content, and tools brings me much closer to the flow I look for in classroom life. It is this flow that lets me know that I am on the right track, and to me it just "feels right." We are engaged in productive learning, things are moving right along, and I feel sometimes, quite frankly, like I am on a wave. I'm not a surfer, but I have a sense of all of us riding a crest when all these elements are in harmony and we share in a collaborative world of learning and teaching.

References

Barnes, Douglas. 1976. *From Communication to Curriculum*. New York: Penguin Books.

Cambourne, Brian. 1988. *The Whole Story*. New York: Scholastic.

Fisher, Bobbi. 1991. *Joyful Learning: A Whole Language Kindergarten*. Portsmouth, NH: Heinemann.

Graves, Donald H. 1989. *Investigate Nonfiction*. Portsmouth, NH: Heinemann.

Heathcote, Dorothy. 1983. "Learning, Knowing and Language in Drama: An Interview with Dorothy Heathcote." *Language Arts* 60: 695–701.

Martin, Nancy. 1976. In *Writing Across the Curriculum Pamphlets*, N. Martin, ed. Portsmouth, NH: Boynton/Cook

National Commission on Social Studies in the Schools. 1989. In "Charting a Course: Social Studies for the 21st Century."

Smith, Frank. 1988. *Joining the Literacy Club*: *Further Essays into Education*. Portsmouth, NH: Heinemann.

CHAPTER ONE

Living in a Generative Curriculum

Pat Cordeiro

Life in a Generative Curriculum

"Mrs. C, Mrs. C—why don't we all pretend to be Pilgrims and write letters back and forth to each other?" Once there was a time in my teaching career when words like this sent me into a panic. I knew what would follow. Eyes flashing, arms waving, the speaker would generate excitement all across the room and other excited voices would chime in: "Yeah, we could all make our paper look old-fashioned with brown paint!" "We could write with seagull feathers like they were quill pens." "Maybe we could dress up!!" "What if we built a real house right here in the room just like the Pilgrims had to do!" "We could make the whole room look just like the Mayflower . . ."

And so it would go. And I would be faced with another mixed blessing. Here were the students, so excited and ready to go, ready to undertake projects on their own (reading and writing incorporated), eager to learn. But I had a plan already in mind, a great deal more limited than theirs, but one that we could do in the afternoons from 1:00 to 2:00, maybe two or three times a week. My plan would also allow us to get through the chapter in the math book that I knew was hard for me and would thus be hard for them. And my plans weren't altogether boring. I had a couple of films in mind, a trade book we could all read together in literature sharing groups, and activities that were, well, more contained than turning the whole room into a model of the Mayflower.

Looking back, it's not hard for me to see the problem with engaging students' minds in *my* plans, plans that engaged *my* mind. It even might have been worse; we never had a social studies text and so I never used the teacher's edition as a guide for planning. To me, that kind of planning is two steps removed from my children and me. At least the things I came up with as long-range plans were only one step removed from the interests and excitements of the children.

11

PAT CORDEIRO

12 ....

Back in my old teaching days, I used to greet such suggestions from children with the same trepidation I felt when anyone suggested putting on a play. It's not easy doing these kinds of things in the classroom. But over the years I found that the only learning that really stuck was the learning that resulted from curriculum activities we generated together.

Over the years I also found that my best teaching and learning came from episodes just like those spontaneous activities children suggested around Pilgrim studies. They weren't always student-generated; sometimes they were more spur of the moment. Sometimes they were inspirations I had on the spot. Sometimes they were brilliant acts of teacher's desperation, born of those times when the filmstrip projector refused to work, or when half the class suddenly had to go and get their ears tested and the rest of us had an hour on our hands. But they were the things that usually worked best. We all got excited, we all were involved, we all participated, and none of us knew what it might lead to next. It was like turning down a path that you've never taken, knowing that you're safe and can always change direction. It was a generative curriculum.

The notion of a generative curriculum (Fisher and Cordeiro 1994; Fisher in press; Cordeiro 1992) put into use by a learner who teaches (Cordeiro 1992–3) is inherent in current whole language philosophies. A generative curriculum is one in which the path and selection of activities that will facilitate learning are not predetermined by the teacher but are generated by all participants in the learning process. A generative curriculum is activated by all learners in the classroom but is initiated and advanced by the teacher, the learner in the classroom who teaches.

The idea of a generative curriculum as a more desirable, more fruitful level for classroom interactions came originally from talking and listening, to my classroom and to my friend, Bobbi Fisher (Fisher and Cordeiro 1994). I have since come to see it as the best way of describing what I did when I tried to make sense out of literacy and social studies.

In a generative curriculum, activities that mark the path of the study are generated by the interaction of all the learners. Activities generated are the result of activities that have gone before. They are not all planned in advance as is so often the case in traditional levels of curriculum, although usually the beginning activity and the ending goal are known so that the curricular path has direction. Too often, activities that are part of "segregated," "coordinated," or "integrated" social studies curricula are decided and organized by the teacher, even before the learners are on the scene. What is deemed good for a particular classroom community is thus the result of mistaken assumptions about the homogeneity of all classroom communities and their assumed match with the material and how it is to be explored.

A generative curriculum validates what good teachers do best— create meaningful learning as needed, usually in company with those who are doing a large part of the learning. I spent many years feeling very guilty. I almost never followed what I had planned. I couldn't help but listen to the children and to that little voice inside me that said, "What you planned in the middle of the night is not the best way to do this—look at those kids over there—they're lost and they don't know what you're talking about." But we are all products of our training and our expectations. And in spite of quite progressive training, my old days as a student were always in the back of my mind: It was my responsibility to decide what we should do, when we should do it, and how long it ought to take. Otherwise, I was conditioned to see myself as a bad planner and a worse implementer. Thus, the constant guilt. I felt disorganized. I felt inadequate. I felt like a poor teacher.

And these feelings occurred in spite of the fact that I could see that these spontaneous and mutually generated interactions were good for my students and good for me. I know that I am a highly organized person, so I should have been easier on myself all those years. But it wasn't until I began exploring the notion of a generative curriculum that I really felt better about the very good learning that was going on around me.

Why a Generative Curriculum is Useful

A generative curriculum is a pathway of learning established by both teachers and children, reflective of learning that has gone before, and responsive to the needs of those involved in it. It makes a good match to beliefs that form the basis of the three strands of this book: social studies, literacy, and whole language.

In these classrooms, children are encouraged to become self-monitoring, self-regulating, and self-propelled. Learning to make good choices is fostered through interaction and activity. Problem solving and decision making are part of the curriculum and are seen as essential elements in every learning experience. Children will expect a reasoned response when they approach you and say, "You know, I've got this great idea for what we could do." Within the theory there is room for learners to be teachers, too.

A generative curriculum allows this engagement to happen by giving learners an active voice in what happens. It frees a teacher to make problem solving and decision making a grounded theory-in-practice by applying them to the life of the classroom itself. Further, not only do children have more control over their classroom lives, but teachers do also. A generative curriculum validates what good teachers do well.

Literacy theory has, since the work of Donald Graves on process writing, recognized the power and necessity for giving learners choice, ownership, and time in the learning process. When teachers and children participate in a curriculum that is mutually generated, these elements can be fulfilled. As important as they are to writers, choice, ownership, and time are equally important to learners in every area. By considering children's needs and suggestions and engaging children in the process of curriculum development, teachers allow them to choose some part of what will be learned and how it will be approached. Activities thus generated in the classroom are owned in every sense of the word by the students because they had such an important hand in creating them. And time is granted for all learners to explore the curriculum thoroughly, so that what is to be learned is given ample opportunity to flourish. Children are encouraged to learn in depth, rather than just in breadth, a feature of successful learning that I learned from studying with Eleanor Duckworth (1987).

A mutually generated curriculum allows a great deal of critical thinking to occur, a goal of the social studies. In developing and managing such a course of study, children become more observant of the value of the activities they do. Because they know they will have a hand in what comes next, they consider more carefully what they are engaged in and whether they would want to do it again. When a generative curriculum is happening in a classroom, children and teachers all have a stake in listening to each other and sharing information, opinions, and ideas. This, in turn, promotes the active participation in democratic citizenship and values, another goal of the social studies.

It always amazed me that, back in my old days, my teachers expected me to learn how to participate in a democratic society by sitting and listening to an authoritarian voice. It's a contradiction in terms to sit and listen about how to be a good citizen. Democratic participation is something that has to be practiced, and a generative curriculum provides the very best opportunity for this because the outcome of discussions affects classroom life so effectively.

What a Generative Curriculum Looks Like

In my example of the study of the Plymouth Pilgrims, a generative curriculum would look very different from how I as a student studied their voyage. Back in my old days, we read about them in our textbook, we probably took at least one test to see if we had learned what we read, and we even may have written one pretend diary entry as if we were one of those unfortunates crossing the North Atlantic in near-winter conditions on a small, cramped boat under sail. We might have completed worksheets to cut out little black hats with big buckles on the front or little brown caps with white around the front. Or we might have just colored in a worksheet picture of Plymouth after we completed some multiplication facts on it. We might have gone to see a Pilgrim play or we even might have put one on, memorizing our lines if we were included in the cast.

As students, we would have been notified of these activities by a listing on the board, and probably by the teacher reminding us. We would have read according to page number assignments, noting when the tests were. Even our diary entry might have appeared on the board as a written assignment. It's funny, I don't really remember my teachers talking to us—I just must have blanked out when they started. And I was a good student. I mostly remember relating to what was written on the board. It was a purely receptive process.

Whether or not we went to the play or put one on would have depended on our teachers. I don't actually remember any Pilgrim plays. I do remember a Nativity scene around Christmastime, but I wasn't in that one. It all was decided in advance by the teachers without any idea that we might have had ideas, too.

One of the things that saddens me about the progress of education is that the school scenario I have just described goes back forty years. But the picture I have painted is also the one reported by my youngest college students today and is the pedagogical dogma in many classrooms I encounter. Sometimes it seems to me that little growth has occurred at all.

The irony of my scenario is that many of us children were going home and "playing Pilgrims" like mad. Children in their playing create generative curricula routinely. Starting with a small idea like "Let's be Pilgrims!," children move through various phases of informal "study." They experiment with ideas they have encountered, play them out to see what they mean, let those ideas lead them to other activities that broaden and personalize their understanding, and even go to the library and read topical books on their own. No one is in charge. Ideas generate other ideas. Children negotiate and explore collaboratively. In play, stories grow, and learning is connected.

Most importantly, in play, children teach themselves. Lev Vygotsky (1978) defines what he calls "the zone of proximal development" as that area of a child's work where instruction, by an adult or a more capable peer, is most fruitful. The "zone" for a child is that region of performance in which the child can problem-solve only because of the presence of help and support:

> It is the distance between the actual developmental level as deter-mined by independent problem solving and the level of potential development as determined through problem solving under adult guidance or in collaboration with more capable peers. (86)

But Vygotsky points out that when children play, they create their own zone of proximal development: "In play a child always behaves beyond his average age, above his daily behavior; in play it is as though he were a head taller than himself" (102).

Do children research the topics they play about? Many college students I talk to report that they did. I remember going to the library to learn new things about a topic we were entranced with. Sometimes we got new information and ideas from grown-ups as they talked to us about our play topics. Often, we drew information from books we encountered, children's stories that we got from libraries and class-rooms. These gave us real people to be, real problems to solve in our informal plays, real knowledge to assimilate and accommodate.

In my classroom, as a teacher, I tried to make use of this quality of children's thinking, this ability to personalize and explore a topic thoroughly and actively. In working with a generative curriculum, I as the teacher knew how we would get started and how we might conclude a unit of study. This beginning and ending gave focus, direction, and coherency beyond simply uniting a collection of activities by a theme.

When I first began working in a generative way, I was afraid that leaving open the possibilities for curriculum development within a topic might lead to a unit of study that looked a little too much like a children's game, one thing leading to another in perhaps too random a fashion. I was afraid that there wouldn't be enough connection and coherency across the unit. Instead, I have found that working within a generative curriculum creates more coherency than I had before. In my old days as a student, the activities we did were united only by the theme: they were all about Plymouth Pilgrims—and we read the textbook. Other than that, one thing did not at all lead to another. We did this, we did that, we approached social studies with what Don Graves once called the "cha-cha-cha" curriculum—do a little over here, do a little over there, cha-cha-cha.

While approaching social studies in a generative way, I found that my students and I considered the connections between things more carefully. We talked, negotiated, and shared ideas. As we studied the Plymouth Pilgrims, I would have some activity ready to get us going. I would learn some topic knowledge at the beginning of the study. We might, for instance, approach the topic analogically, talking about why people move and then investigating our own experiences with moving from one place to another. I might arrange for my students to move to a strange environment in the course of the school day so that we could have a personal experience with what the Plymouth Pilgrims went through. I would have this experience with them, although I would be the engineer, also. I think there's nothing more powerful than feeling something yourself to help understand what others experienced in history.

The students and I would both know that we were heading toward studying the Pilgrims, and shortly they would begin to take over control of how we would go about learning this topic. We might have a series of activities that would seem logical to us and that would lead us from examining one aspect of the Plymouth Pilgrim experience to another, giving us insight about why they did what they did. As the unit proceeded, we would share knowledge of how the unit would end, but in a broad-based way. For example, we might know that this particular unit was going to end with a schoolwide sharing, or with a written research project to be placed in the school library, or we might be finishing the unit with a trip to some place like Plymouth. The culminating activity would always tie things together for a bigger purpose than "doing it for the teacher," like teaching younger students what we knew or preparing ourselves for a trip.

As the unit proceeded, students would take control of the course of study. Just as teachers must have greater control and centrality in the fall of the school year and then gradually give it over to students as spring approaches so they may become independent, self-directing learners, so it happens in a unit of study. I would hold most of the knowledge at the beginning and take most of the control. As a generative curriculum study would proceed, students would take over more and more of the responsibility for directing how, why, and when things happened, and they would become the primary knowledge-holders. I believe, as a student of process writing instruction, that there is nothing more powerful than teaching somebody else something you know and they don't. By spring I try to be the primary learner in the classroom, giving my students both an audience and model for this process.

Once I began thinking about a triad of learning areas as linked— social studies, literacy, and whole language together—and I envisioned them as a source of flow in our classroom life, a generative curriculum came naturally. It was a type of letting go, like riding the crest of a wave. I found it very exciting. It let the students and me be the very best, creative, and enthusiastic learners we could be. And when voices chimed in, "What if we pretended to be Pilgrims . . . we could write letters and make packing lists . . . what do you suppose they had to take with them? Mrs. C, where we can we find out what the Pilgrims packed when they traveled?" I shared in the happening. Together we set about learning.

References

Cordeiro, Pat. 1992–3. "Becoming a Learner Who Teaches." *Teachers Networking: The Whole Language Newsletter* 12 (Winter): 1, 3–5.

———. 1992. *Whole Learning: Whole Language and Content in the Upper Elementary Grades.* Katonah, NY: Richard C. Owen.

Duckworth, Eleanor. 1987. *"The Having of Wonderful Ideas" and Other Essays on Teaching and Learning.* New York: Teachers College Press.

Fisher, Bobbi. March 1995. *Thinking and Learning Together: Curriculum and Community in a Primary Classroom.* Portsmouth NH: Heinemann.

Fisher, Bobbi, and Pat Cordeiro, eds. 1994. *Primary Voices.* Urbana, IL: National Council of Teachers of English.

Vygotsky, Lev. 1978. *Mind in Society: The Development of Higher Psychological Processes.* Cambridge, MA: Harvard University Press.

Bobbi has always been interested in engaging children in what they're curious about because that's how she remembers that she and her friends learned best. They were always playing. They had a lot of props and a lot of books, and it all got them really interested in learning. As a teacher, Bobbi translated this into setting up structures so that children could choose what they wanted to do. Working within those structures, children create and learn. Bobbi says, "I've always been in awe of what they actually do when they choose and learn."

Bobbi began making changes by initiating writing and writing process in her classroom. Children wrote and she conferenced with them. She found it much more interesting than the basal reading groups she thought she was supposed to be doing but never quite could get going. She says, "Everybody was interested in what they were doing. No matter what their literacy was, all seemed excited." There was no grouping because she had eliminated ability groups. As the children explored literacy through writing, they enjoyed what they were doing. One reported, "I didn't do any work all day!" They had written all day. Bobbi says, "Everyone was equal."

She found writing to be a successful "way in" to literacy because "Writing was them doing their own ideas." She did have some story starters hanging up in the classroom, things like "If I were a butterfly . . . ," but kids wrote their own ideas. Bobbi says, "I guess I'm an independent person and I like to do my own stuff—that's how I learn, how I get excited. I do best when nobody makes me do things. I wanted that for kids—to be self-motivated, self-directed. Let them be."

She remembers the day when somebody walked into her second-grade classroom and put a pile of books on a table, saying "Here are your workbooks for reading." She remembers thinking, "Who said I wanted these?" She did use them a little bit, and there was a lot of talk among other teachers about getting reading groups set. Bobbi thought, "Why am I doing this?" She used to jokingly ask another teacher, a friend of hers, "Do I have to do reading groups today?" and the other teacher would reply, "No, you don't." When she did do them, she tried to get them done by 10:30 in the morning so she could get on with the activities she felt were best. She felt like that was when the day really began. She says, "Now my day begins when the kids come in."

A key for Bobbi in her change process has been having two administrators she trusted. She felt they believed she would do a good job and do the best for kids. She adds, "That was their nature and no mixed messages."

The most important issue for Bobbi is trust. She says, "When I'm trusted I trust the kids to learn, I trust myself. It goes around and around. I trust that when kids are engaged they are learning, even when I may not know what it is they're learning. And I don't have to teach it for them to learn it."

CHAPTER TWO

Things Take Off: Note Taking in the First Grade

Bobbi Fisher

On the first day of school I put a sign in an empty aquarium. It asked, "What could live here?" Alex responded with a picture of a snake. On the second day Chuckie found a tomato worm and we made a habitat for it. This initiated an interest in small animals and things just started taking off from there.

During workshop time when children choose from a variety of activities, a group of children decided to learn about animal classification and made a series of mobiles, each displaying animals from the appropriate group. At silent reading they perused nonfiction books about animals. I read *Benny's Animals* (Selsam 1966), and the children started cutting out pictures of animals, sorting them according to classification, and pasting them on posters.

We decided to get hamsters as our classroom pet. When the mother had eleven babies, the children recorded their observations of the hamsters' actions. We published a special edition of our classroom newspaper about the hamsters.

Victor discovered ants on the floor near where we keep our lunches. He and some others put out some food to see how many ants it would attract and where the ants came from. It was all part of a generative curriculum (Cordeiro 1992).

What Is a Generative Curriculum?

In my first-grade classroom, a generative curriculum encourages the natural learning environment, in which one focus of inquiry generates another, interests are initiated and pursued throughout the year, and connections and relationships are continually made. The cumulative effect is an environment in which learning is ongoing, dynamic, and related. Life and learning are seen as a whole in which a book, a topic,

21

areas of study, an art project, or a science experiment reflects and suggests the entire curriculum of life, just as tiny holograms each contain the much larger whole object within themselves.

A generative curriculum helps learners apply the processes of reading, writing, speaking, listening, art, music, drama, and mathematics to gain meaning and understanding from the content areas of social studies and science—with children's literature playing a central role in integrating these processes and content. There is always a flow or interplay between content learning and process learning. We learn content through process, and process through content. The two are not separated.

List Making and Note Taking

One of the roles of the teacher in a generative curriculum is to offer the children opportunities to develop skills and strategies necessary for acquiring independence and control of their learning through writing, within the authentic inquiry situations of a generative curriculum. In my classroom I introduce the process of note taking as a tool for pursuing content interests in more depth.

I introduce note taking early in the year and continue building upon demonstrations of possibilities, which increase in complexity as the children's reading, writing, and research sophistication grows. I explain that note taking helps us quickly record what is important so we can remember it for later use. Therefore, I add, we just want to write down the important words or draw a simple picture. I encourage the children to draw as well as write because drawing includes those students who are not comfortable with invented spelling yet, and validates those who like to express themselves visually. Usually the children take notes on a blank piece of paper on a clipboard, which allows them the flexibility of working on the floor, at tables, or as they walk about.

We start note taking at the beginning of the year by making lists. For example, I asked the children to make a list of all the animals that they would like the class to consider getting for the aquarium cage. Then, as they shared their suggestions during group time, I made a master list on chart paper. They were encouraged to add ideas and make corrections to their lists. Discussion continued for a few weeks as we reread the master list, marked it up, crossed out the suggestions we had eliminated, and recorded several consensus votes.

We also take notes during learning walks. When we went on a nature walk around the school yard, the children worked in twos. Each pair had a clipboard, paper, and pencil, and had to decide how to share the materials and writing responsibilities. Sometimes during workshop a pair of children walk around the school with clipboards and record information for a social studies or science inquiry study. For example, they have made lists of properties (shapes, sizes, color, texture), the five senses, environmental print, and things that magnetize.

As the children develop many of the conventions of list making and note taking, their lists become more organized and easier to read. They might number the items, use bullets, underline, and use arrows to organize their thoughts.

Note Taking from Books

A particular challenge for me as a first-grade teacher is to provide ways for the children to obtain and record new information from printed material, primarily books. As emergent and beginning readers, they haven't gained the fluency needed to read independently the texts that they can understand and respond to orally. Note taking is one strategy that helps form a bridge between reading and writing as I support the group and individual children by reading to and with them, demonstrating, and encouraging writing.

The following three examples involve note taking from books and generate from earlier list-making experiences. It is important to keep in mind that note taking is not a goal in itself, but a tool to help us learn about authentic topics of inquiry. For example, the African study described below, which concentrated on taking notes from pictures and oral text, was part of committee work to plan projects for the rest of the class. The schoolwide water theme, which involved using an index to take specific types of notes from books, culminated in a song about rivers to share with the school. The Japan study, which involved writing an original text from notes, produced a book about Japan.

Committee Work in an African Study

ESTABLISHING COMMITTEES   On the day before the December vacation, I told the children that we would be studying Africa when we returned to school in January. I introduced the topic before vacation so they could think about what we would be studying, and so I could do some planning that would be generated from their interests. We brainstormed the following list, which I wrote on chart paper, of what we might like to learn:

- Animals
- Mummies
- Temples
- How the people make things
- Scorpion herd
- Languages
- Houses
- Clothing
- Writing
- How is it different and similar to us
- Food
- Sculpture and art
- Pharaohs' names
- Books
- Black and white people

During vacation I used the brainstorming list to identify topics for six committees that would form the organizational framework for our theme immersion (Manning, Manning, and Long 1994): animals, clothing, the arts, food, houses, and languages. I purposely made the topics concrete because I wanted us to be able to find information and create projects easily. (Native languages didn't fit these criteria, but throughout the year several children had expressed interest in learning about languages, and I wanted to honor and encourage that interest.)

During the first two days after vacation, as a way of preparing the children to choose a committee, I read five books about Africa: *The Day of Ahmed's Secret* (Heide 1990)—a story set in modern-day Cairo; *The Village of Round and Square Houses* (Grifalconi 1990)—a story about a girl in a village in Ghana; *How the Guinea Fowl Got Her Spots* (Knutson 1990)—a folk tale set in the African Plains; *Who's in Rabbit's House* (Aaredema 1977)—another folk tale; and the first chapter of *A New True Book: Africa* (Georges 1986). We talked about what we noticed and could learn about Africa from these different kinds of books.

On the third day I explained the letter they would be taking home to their parents about our African study. They were to discuss the committee possibilities with them, and bring back a paper with their first and second choices. This action informed and involved the parents and required the children to make an initial commitment to the area that interested them the most. Each committee would be responsible for planning learning projects on its topic for the rest of the class. Here is a copy of my letter:

January 5

Dear Parents,

For the next six weeks we will be studying Africa as part of Sudbury's first-grade social studies curriculum. Before the holiday vacation the children and I talked about what we would like to learn, and I have summarized our list into the following six topics: animals, clothing, food, houses, languages, and the arts.

We are now in the process of forming study committees. Each committee will research its topic, arrange activities, and plan ways to present information to the rest of the class. Although we have talked about each topic in class, I am asking that the children make their final committee choice after discussing the project with you. Please help them to write their first and second choice on the form below and bring it to school tomorrow.

If you can help in any of the following ways, please let me know:
• Loan artifacts, pictures, books, etc.
• Help with a cooking project.
• Help with an art project.
• Help make adinkra cloths at the craft center.

Sincerely,

Bobbi Fisher

On Friday we formed the committees. I made a graph with the six choices and wrote each child's name on a Post-it so we could move the names around easily. The children put their name on the column of their first choice. Since no one had chosen languages and only one person had selected clothing, we decided to eliminate those as committees and just work with four. I also felt that four would be easier for me to facilitate, and I wanted the children to be on the committees they really desired. At first, the remaining four committees were uneven, and several children were willing to change. Finally I asked if everyone was satisfied, adding that once the committees were formed, it would be difficult to change. A few more switches were made, and the class agreed that having three committees of six members, and one of four, was manageable.

NOTE TAKING   Note taking actively involved the committee members in the process of obtaining information on which to plan their projects. Each time I read a book about Africa to the class, one member from each committee took notes on the group's topic. Everyone did this at least once, and some children volunteered to take notes on transportation and clothing as well. I reread the original books, as well as several others. These included folk tales, story books, and information books.

In preparation for note taking, the students selected to take notes that day wrote their name, committee name, and book title on a plain piece of paper on a clipboard. As I read, they wrote and/or drew pictures of anything they noticed or heard about their subject. Throughout the reading, classmates and I made suggestions and discussed possible entries, and committee members helped each other. There was a lively interplay among all the children, but especially by the designated note takers.

PUTTING IT ALL TOGETHER   After about two weeks of reading and note taking, each committee met with me. Using their notes and many books, they planned the following projects for the rest of the class. Almost everyone participated in all of the projects.

Houses

- The group made a mural of *Ahmed's Secret*, and a mural and diorama of *The Village of Round and Square Houses*. They taught the rest of the class how to make round and square houses out of paper.

Animals

- Everyone made an animal with clay. The class planned this project with the art teacher.
- The animals committee collaborated with the houses group and drew animals on their murals.

Art

- Everyone made a mask depicting one of the characters in *Who's in Rabbit's House?* Later we acted it out as I read the story.
- They made an adinkra cloth at the school craft center with the help of parents.
- Everyone contributed a section of a decorative border for the murals.

Food

- The group looked at some cookbooks and decided on four recipes. Parents organized the cooking. Everyone had a taste.

Things Take Off: Note Taking in the First Grade

.... 27

Song Writing in a Study About Water

In March note taking became an important step in creating the song "I Like the Rivers" (an innovation on "I Like the Rain" by Claude Belanger [1988]), to sing to the school as part of a schoolwide theme on water. First, the whole class wrote the chorus, "I Like the River," and then small groups wrote different verses.

For the chorus, I read aloud sections from several books that told the characteristics of rivers. I demonstrated how to use an index and skim text to locate specific information. Using the 3-by-5-inch notebooks the children had brought from home earlier in the year, they wrote down key words that we might use for the song, while I wrote them on the chart paper. Discussion followed as we determined the most important attributes of a river and put the words into verse.

For this water study, the class was divided into four study groups named after the Amazon, Ganges, Mississippi, and Nile rivers. "I like the Amazon," "I like the Ganges," "I like the Mississippi," and "I like the Nile," became the first lines for each verse.

I worked individually with the groups during workshop time, incorporating what I had demonstrated when the entire class wrote the chorus. We looked through information books about rivers, locating the name of the river in the index and putting markers at each page. I helped the children skim and read for information to include in their song. As we selected important facts and/or concepts describing the river, a group member wrote them down. Then we used the list to create the words for the song. I wrote the lines on a chart and the group illustrated them with markers. Later each group taught their verse to the class and explained the information they had included.

Writing a Class Book During a Japan Study

In May the class was involved in a study of Japan to prepare for a first-grade Japan Day Festival and as self-selected inquiry projects. Five children had picked Japan for their inquiry topic. I decided that we would make a class book about Japan, focusing on the skills and strategies involved in skimming a text to gain information for note taking, and on writing our own text from our notes.

The children sat on the rug with clipboards, pencils, and paper, and shared among themselves the eight copies I had of *A New True Book: Japan* (Jacobsen 1982). First they looked through the book, paying attention to the table of contents and index, and talking among themselves about the topics they wanted to include in our book. We decided on three chapters: "The Land," "Food," and "Education," which we wrote as a class the next three days.

First, everyone wrote "The Land" for a heading, and as we read the text together, we talked about the important ideas and discussed what key words we should write. I wrote them on a big piece of paper and the children copied them. Some added other words and/or drew pictures.

Next we read the notes and put the words into our own sentences, which I wrote on a chart. Everyone was required to take the notes, but they had the choice of copying the text as I wrote. Most of the children who had chosen Japan for their inquiry topic opted to do so.

The charts became part of the decorations for the Japan Day Festival in the gym. I put the text on the computer and everyone had a copy of the book.

Summary

These examples of note taking are tools for learning within a generative curriculum. The children were introduced to some of the skills and strategies involved in note taking: using an index and table of contents; examining pictures and photographs for information; listing the important words when recording information; and writing a text from a list. They used these skills within the context of authentic inquiry: to plan projects so their classmates could learn about Africa; to write a song about rivers to share with the school; and to make a wall chart for the Japan Day Festival.

As the children developed these note-taking skills, they became more and more able to work independently and to control the direction of their own interests. They were able to follow up on ideas, which then generated new topics of inquiry to pursue. They were able to work more confidently and independently as they generated their own curriculum. In other words, for them, "Things just took off."

Lindsay was indignant when she started to take notes about plants and realized that the book she chose didn't have an index. She made her own Table of Contents for the book, and then went on with her report. Luke made a list of what he liked about the new school playground, and then wrote an original song, entitled—what else?—"I Like the Playground." Greg rooted cuttings from an ivy plant for everyone in the class and made lots of lists to keep track of his project.

As for Assessment...

The purpose of the note taking described in this chapter was to help the children develop a skill and a tool that would support them in gaining knowledge and making sense of new learning. I assessed their progress in learning this skill in two ways: by periodically assessing the children's work over time, and by daily kidwatching.

Throughout the year I regularly evaluated the children's work by looking at samples of their notes, which were part of their writing portfolios, and comparing representative samples of earlier notes with later ones to assess progress in the children's understanding and use of note taking. I found in general that as the year went on their notes became better organized and more concise.

I also evaluated progress by kidwatching during group time, when we did most of the note taking. As I listened to the children's responses and watched what they did, I made adjustments when they appeared confused or disengaged. For example, when a child kept asking what to do next, I paired him with a helpful partner. After the first note taking session on the African books, I noticed that some of the children's papers were disorganized and hard to read. I then demonstrated how to number a list and suggested that the children give it a try.

I knew that learning had occurred when I noticed children beginning to use note taking for their own authentic purposes. Christian provided a specific example of this one day as he worked on a research topic on snakes. He told me that he wasn't going to copy everything from the book; he planned to write down only the important words that he would need when he wrote his report.

References

Aaredema, V. 1977. *Who's in Rabbit's House?* New York: Dial.

Belanger, C. 1988. *I Like the Rain*. Crystal Lake, IL: Rigby.

Cordeiro, P. 1992. *Whole Learning: Whole Language and Content in the Upper Elementary Grades*. Katonah, NY: Richard C. Owen.

Georges, D. V. 1986. *A New True Book: Africa*. Chicago: Children's Press.

Grifalconi, A. 1990. *The Village of Round and Square Houses*. New York: Little Brown.

Heide, F. 1990. *The Day of Ahmed's Secret*. New York: Lothrop.

Jacobsen, K. 1982. *A New True Book: Japan*. Chicago: Children's Press.

Knutson, N. 1990. *How the Guinea Fowl Got Her Spots*. New York: Carolrhona.

Manning, G., M. Manning, and R. Long. 1994. *Theme Immersions*. Portsmouth, NH: Heinemann.

Selsam, M. 1966. *Benny's Animals*. New York: Harper.

Pat Reflects—

When I read Bobbi's account of the first graders working so meaningfully with note taking, I am struck by the distance between her account and my memories of "learning note taking" in junior high. We were taught to take notes on topics we weren't studying in any class, and note taking was taught under the curriculum heading of "study skills." To my best recollection, somebody read a section of text aloud, the teacher wrote notes on the board, and we all copied what the teacher wrote. It was, at best, a lesson in handwriting, and not a very good one at that, for the teacher usually went fast to replicate what would happen when we were trying to take notes during a lecture in preparation for a test.

I suspect that, like Bobbi's first graders, many of us only learned this particular "study skill" when we really had to—when we were in a heated situation in which we had to capture information and did so in whatever fashion we could. And probably a lot of kids simply never did learn how to take notes in an effective and efficient manner that worked for them.

As Bobbi points out, taking notes is a tool for learning. Never an end in itself, it serves us well only when it works. And it works only when it works for each of us individually. Historically, we have often referred to writing and reading as "tools," but rightfully they are processes and particular applications of them are best referred to as "tools." Just as using a lever is a process and particular kinds of levers, like crowbars, are tools, so using writing is a process and particular kinds of writing, like note taking, are tools.

When children are engaged over time in activities like note taking in a meaningful way, as we see here in Bobbi's account, they develop a style of "tool use" that suits them and works well for communicating with peers. As Bobbi says, children begin to need ways of organizing their lists, such as bullets and numbering. Some of these note taking conventions are ones that Bobbi suggests, others are ones that arise spontaneously from the users themselves as they become more adept at manipulating the tools in useful and efficient ways.

Young children are not usually exposed to the idea of note taking. School teachers and administrators generally think of it as a skill that will only be needed when students are in the "content" grades. But as Bobbi points out, first graders, and even kindergartners, have as many needs for taking notes as older children do. All the grades are, in fact, "content" grades, for children are always studying about the world. More importantly, as Bobbi points out, note taking forms a link between reading and writing and therefore serves many purposes for children in their emergent literacy. Note taking enables children to transfer ideas from one medium to another, whether they take notes with words or pictures and graphics.

Finally, Bobbi reminds me that one of the greatest powers of working within a generative curriculum is the cumulative, overall effect. In establishing a generative curriculum in our classrooms, it is not enough to stop at simply having the children help us with the planning. Generating ideas for what to do next is only part of what makes a generative curriculum work. The deeper, more far-reaching goal is a generative environment, one that supplies resources and structures for an ongoing generative curriculum. And no one is better at establishing that in the classroom than Bobbi.

Reflecting on the changes over time in her life as a teacher reminded Sandra of how complex yet developmental those changes were. She taught first grade for six years and then left teaching for a while. When she came back, she taught preschool before returning to first and then second grade. She found that her experiences teaching preschool made a great difference in her first-grade teaching. She says, "I approached the curriculum and classroom structuring in a different way." She found that she no longer gave the children routine tasks, and she felt uncomfortable with most teacher-designed groupings of children. She felt more concerned with the children's interests than she had been before and listened to "how they wanted to express their learning."

These changes weren't instantaneous but were accompanied by Sandra also becoming more proactive in her school. Report cards were a problem for primary teachers at that time, so she served on committees to influence decisions about assessment. Eventually she contributed to every area of the curriculum by working on committees.

She also began giving workshops to other teachers and found that this was perhaps the single most influential factor in continuing change and growth for her. It caused her to attend more to research findings, by taking courses and reading professional books and journals. She began to search for justifications for the changes that were coming naturally in her classroom.

Sandra believes now that teachers should be encouraged to present workshops, and she finds nothing more important than the thinking, telling, reflecting, and sharing that this experience promotes. She would like to see teachers not as mere "receivers of a smorgasbord of learning," but as thinkers who decide what they want to learn and zero in on what they think is important. In giving new workshops, she finds new things to research herself.

Sandra sees herself as reflective, having "given [herself] permission to reflect." She recognizes that a teacher has to give up something in order to have the time to reflect, but feels that the teacher and the class get so much more out of learning when planning comes from reflection.

In the fall of 1994, Sandra began a new life as "Staff Leader"/Principal in her school. This school is a special place that, in Sandra's words, "epitomizes a generative curriculum because of a self-selected creative staff. It is a school that was itself generated from the interests and professional ideals of the staff. The same energy is found in curricular development in the whole school and in the classrooms."

Here in Sandra's chapter, we see that same generative energy at work in her second grade.

CHAPTER THREE

Social Studies and Literacy in the Second Grade

Sandra Wilensky

Introduction: Historical Fiction in the Classroom

If we ask ourselves for our rationale in teaching history, a major component of social studies, we find it is in order to understand peoples of today—both nationally and internationally—and to learn the lessons of the past, so that we will not repeat human atrocities. We as educators have a responsibility in this business of ethics and morality—developing values. After all, it's the youth we teach today who will be problem solving in and designing our future world. Children need to be developing their "voice" at an early age and gaining a sense of a larger context through which to view and interpret their own experiences. In my classroom, I ask children to express their voice as in writing to the president (see Figure 3–1). I use historical fiction to allow children to examine different historical periods and to relate to the characters—to see themselves as a part of history.

The school system I teach in has defined "Communities: Past and Present" as the content to be studied in second grade. With this as a guideline, I developed a structure through which we would study communities in American History, follow a time line, and become familiar with the periods by learning about their people. Through a series of read-alouds of historical fiction (I also read nonfiction and other fiction), we got to know well ten diverse characters (ages eight to ten) and their families. Since the physical science part of our curriculum is "Systems" (such as electricity and gears), which integrates nicely with the Industrial Revolution, that became an area I planned to highlight with events and activities designed to integrate the curriculum. Other highlighted topics, including slavery, were generated from the group's natural questions and interests.

This vehicle of historical fiction created shared experiences of living in the past for our classroom community. We lived through the

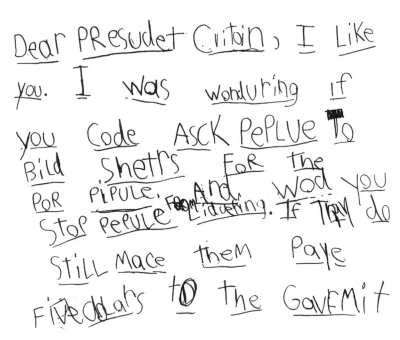

FIG. 3–1   Letter to the president

characters and their triumphs over life's challenges. We moved through the time of Columbus's invasion of the Native Americans' land to today's issue of homelessness. We examined our town and larger community, both past and present, and made time capsules to leave information about our lives for the future. Our characters settled new lands, were slaves, emigrated to the west, immigrated to America, marched for women's rights, had sisters who worked in a mill, took care of family at home during a war, lived in an airport, and had mail-order mothers. These characters were interesting and their stories were real and exciting. I did not need to plan the excitement—it was intrinsic. The curriculum flowed naturally and with meaning.

I read these books aloud during meeting time, as the children sat gathered on the rug. Most often the children followed along with their own copies. This provided us with a daily wealth of shared and meaningful experiences from which we as a class, in small groups, and individually, generated our work and our curriculum—social studies, science, writing, art, discussion, and projects. This method of whole group reading allowed everyone, regardless of reading ability, to participate equally—a basic premise of my teaching philosophy. Many children read the books again by themselves after we had finished as a class. Some chose to reread right away, and some children revisited the characters, time period, and ideas much later in the year.

Classroom Structure and Environment

My second-grade classroom had several rectangular tables for four to six students, several half-round tables for two people, and several desks for individuals who chose to work alone. There were two carpeted areas for using blocks or meeting, and open shelves and closets for storing all supplies. A workbench and science table housed tools and equipment. Each day began with meeting time and then was divided into writing workshop, study groups, math workshop (which involved the introduction of new concepts and skill practice time), and choice/project time. The children moved around, talked, got their own materials, and chose where to sit. We lived and worked in the classroom together. I moved among the children as a member of the group. Beyond this basic framework, the structure of the classroom was, in many ways, generated by the books we were reading at a given time, and the projects that were inspired by the books.

In the fall, we constructed a cabin in our classroom from a four-by-four-by-six-foot wooden crate. It held many artifacts brought in by the children and me—a hand-crocheted coverlet, candle molds, an old razor, irons, a bed warmer, an oxen yoke, old school books, and a basket of fleece and carders. As we read and got to know Sarah in *The Courage of Sarah Noble* (Dalgliesh 1987), children added a fireplace and tables constructed from cardboard. It became a popular place to read and to think about what life was like before running water and electricity.

If the purpose of Social Studies/History is to broaden our children's world and increase appreciation and understanding of its peoples, then we need to bring the children into the context of the time period they are studying. They should then be able to make more thoughtful expressions and demonstrations of their learning. And they do. One day in the fall after reading *Sarah, Plain and Tall* (MacLachlan 1987) and taking a class field trip to the Little Red School House at the Wayside Inn in Sudbury, Massachusetts, stories about colonial times started appearing during writing time (see Figure 3–2). There were stories— fictional and nonfictional accounts—that demonstrated a knowledge of much factual information and expressed an appreciation and an understanding of what life was like in colonial times. Handcrafted slates and old-fashioned beginning reading books appeared in the cabin.

When the main character's father in *It's Only Goodbye* (Gross

SANDRA WILENSKY

36 ....

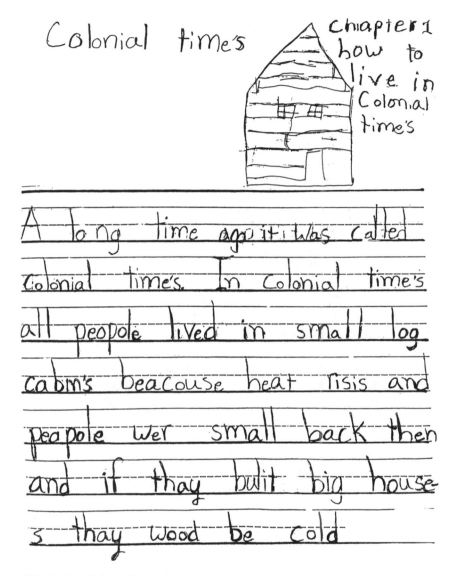

Colonial times

Chapter 1
how to live in Colonial times

A long time ago it was called Colonial times. In Colonial times all peopole lived in small log cabin's beacouse heat risis and peopole wer small back then and if thay buit big houses thay wood be cold

FIG. 3–2 Colonial times story

1992) was thrown in the brig, the children empathized and were eager to problem-solve his situation. When Lila's grandmother in *A Long Way To Go* (Oneal 1990) was arrested for picketing for the womens' right to vote and her parents were embarrassed, the children empathized with Lila's feelings of mixed loyalties. Although these situations were such that eight-year-old children in 1993 had no first-, second-, or thirdhand experience of, they could relate to the emotions, feelings, and strength of the characters. The real ice tongs in the cabin helped them imagine life during World War I, when Theodore in *Hero over Here* (Kudlinski 1992) was the man in charge of his family at ten years old. The characters were role models for values of courage, fortitude, strength of conviction, strong family love, individuality, and faith in humankind. The students continuously exhibited inquisitiveness, intellectual pursuit, resourcefulness, and individual expression. Writing, reading, talking, making projects, playacting, building with Legos and blocks, presenting puppet shows, and artifact constructions were all vehicles for self-explanation. Finished products were shared.

Growth of the Curriculum

Our focus in the classroom soon became slavery and the underground railroad. *Next Stop Freedom* (Hoobler and Hoobler 1991) and its central character, Emily, inspired much serious interest, thought, and discussion about human rights and injustice. During project time, plantations complete with slave quarters were built from blocks and Legos. Emily's cornhusk doll prompted a class project of making such dolls. Her thirty-pound bags of cotton offered challenging math opportunities and discussion. Replicas of the blue book used by the slave owner's children with their teacher appeared in our cabin.

Questions about what might really be in the cabin during a particular time and what didn't fit during other time periods led to rich conversation. This provided excellent opportunities for the children to reflect and demonstrate their new understandings, and for me to assess and appreciate their learning. However, it wasn't necessary or of any interest to the children to remove anything from the cabin; what belonged at an appropriate time was only a point for discussion. Children do not need or want everything tied up in neat little packages. In fact, they seemed to like and benefit from being allowed to cycle and recycle through previous curriculum themes and topics. Perhaps they need to do that in order to make their own necessary connections (Duckworth 1987) for real learning to take place.

We moved on to the Industrial Revolution, and as we read together the book *Hannah's Fancy Notions* (Ross 1992), artifacts appeared on a table near the cabin—tangible sources of the meaning for the children of the times. There was a band box, a hat, a hat pin, an old Singer sewing machine, and old photographs of classmates' relatives. The classroom was beginning to look like a museum. Life-sized silhouettes of the characters we had met in our readings lined one wall of our room. Again, the children had been able to relate the experiences of the character, Hannah, to their own. She had become real to them and had enabled them to gain a better understanding of the period.

As we began talking about the twentieth century, the children became interested in how much things cost when I was their age. Old *Life* magazines provided a glimpse into the forties, fifties, and sixties—the years of my childhood and young adulthood. They discovered through another collection of older books and magazines (early 1900s) how the Machine Age changed the world. Filmstrips and books from every area library were available for the children's use. Hats and old magazines were added to our cabin collection.

The cabin was not the only structure to aid us in our understandings of the characters in the books we were reading. Our classroom became a factory when we made Jacob's Ladders (old-fashioned toys from pieces of wood about the size of a playing card, connected to ribbon). One math challenge was to figure out how much wood class member Kyle's dad needed to buy in order for twenty-five children to make one Jacob's Ladder each. They calculated with a cardboard sample of one piece of wood. Children were sprawled all over the room with poster board, large pieces of paper taped together, rulers, yardsticks, and pens. It was an engrossing process for them and for me—a real problem to solve.

As the factory project began, we created an assembly line with old lunch trays containing pieces of sandpaper of various grains and pieces of precut wood to sand. Children sanded and passed the wood to the next person to sand again. This process continued until the wood got to the last person in line and was smooth. The sanded pieces of wood were then placed in sealed baggies with the necessary pieces of ribbon. The next step—putting on the ribbon—was accomplished by children working with a partner.

The factory study groups went on for several weeks. As groups, the children initiated various projects, decided when they were finished, culminated their work with a presentation to the class, and invited questions and comments from peers (much in the same way as in our writing workshops). They often included explanations of why something was the way it was. One group presented a Lego waterwheel and reported that "the first waterwheel didn't work, and so we did it this way." The process was clearly as important as the product to the children, and the freedom to use the classroom in whatever way their work required was liberating for them.

One group, however, never presented a finished product. In their

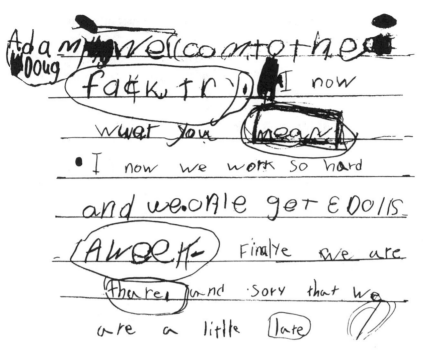

FIG. 3–3   One student's contribution to the play

own assessment, they stated that they couldn't succeed in working together. They were writing a play, a difficult task for second graders, and
found it impossible to weave their separate scripts together (see Figure
3–3). The student teacher and I offered help; however, they insisted on
trying to resolve the problem themselves. Eventually their production
petered out slowly as each of the children lost interest. It was too hard. I
accepted this and did not push them to complete their production.

The natural dissolution of this group's project, which I allowed to
unfold, parallels what happens to us as adults sometimes when we risk
and bite off something really ambitious. But it is difficult for us as
teachers to accept that projects can "fail." Those of us who were trained
in the "factory model" of learning and teaching still have the "complete
the textbook" mentality creeping into our new understandings of how
children learn. We need to trust ourselves and the children to make
appropriate choices (including the choice of when to persevere and
when to quit) and then respect the decision. I relate this experience for
the very reason that I'm writing this chapter: learning requires taking
risks. Everything in life doesn't turn out as planned, in or out of the
classroom. The important thing is to be flexible and to encourage each
other to try.

Choice and Experimentation: Learning as an Ongoing Experience

Choice has always been important in my classroom. We all appreciate having something to say about how we invest our time. I never choose writing topics or books to read for the children. Their work is theirs in a profound sense—they own it. They decide to edit, add, delete, or complete a piece of writing or project. Just the other day I received a letter from one of the children who was in my class last year. After telling me about her summer vacation to Washington, D.C., she said, "The book I'm reading is *Charlie and the Chocolate Factory* [Dahl 1984]. It's a good fit." The term "ownership" has been used a lot lately in education—particularly about writing. As teachers we need to trust ourselves and our students to make good choices. They will and do— if we allow it to happen.

Choice time for at least an hour every day is a time for projects in our classroom. Sometimes I have made guidelines, such as, "Today we will begin small group projects having to do with the mills or factories. You can do whatever you want having to do with mills and factories." When beginning these projects, students discussed ideas, made sketches, generated lists of supplies needed, and wrote descriptions of their factories (see Figure 3–4). The children scouted around for available stuff in the classroom and integrated what was available with what was on their lists (see Figure 3–5). Their resourcefulness was amazing. Items came in from home to supplement their construction supplies and props. I often didn't know who brought what in. Items just appeared and belonged to the group.

During a series of such times, one group made a Lego factory, complete with waterwheel and large storage silo; another group made a crayon factory constructed from cardboard, including stage coach vehicles for delivery of people and goods; still another built a multilevel car factory constructed with blocks. One group wrote and produced a play about mill girls and another a play on the workings of the mill. As the groups constructed their mills and factories, they diligently took apart, revised, and rebuilt their plans to accommodate their new understanding. These projects were entirely theirs, and the groups were self-selected. Occasionally I would set a maximum size to the groups, but I never controlled who worked with whom. I very rarely was consulted on how to do something. They valued their own ideas and would persevere in efforts to improve something to the group's satisfaction.

As we moved through the our country's history, we kept track of times past on a time line we created—with dinosaurs on one end and

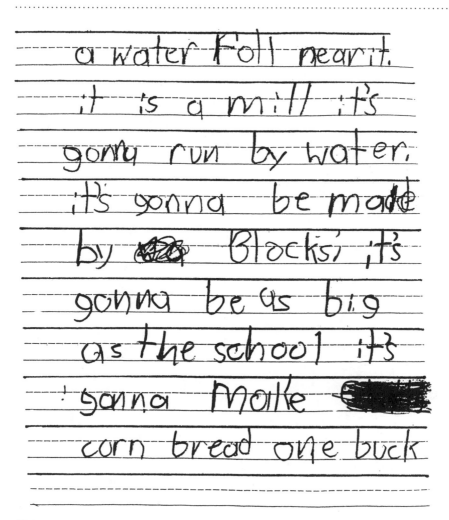

FIG. 3–4   *Student description of a factory*

our second-grade class on the other end. As we placed file cards with drawings on the time line, there was always much discussion about what happened before and after the character lived or the event happened. This was an ongoing and natural context-organizing activity. Often, during choice time, the children would talk with each other about the characters in the books they were reading and where their lives would be marked on the time line.

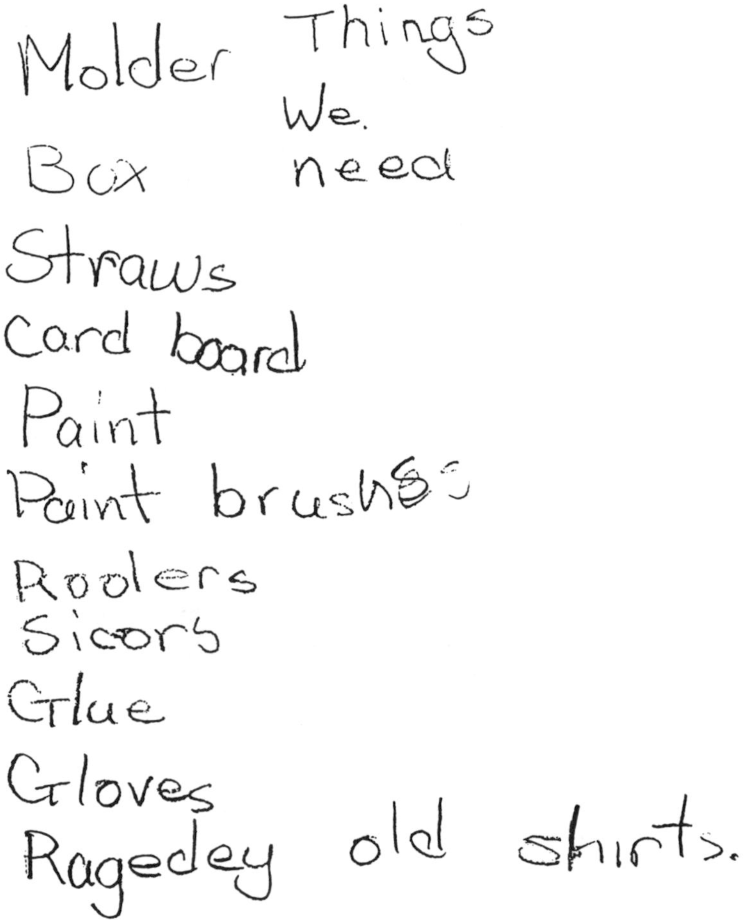

Molder Things
We.
Box need
Straws
Card board
Paint
Paint brushes
Roolers
Sicors
Glue
Gloves
Ragedey old shirts.

FIG. 3–5   *Student list of supplies*

Historical characters and their times were kept alive in another way—through new pieces of the children's writing. One child, Elissa, continued her interest in slavery most of the year. Her story themes often were about acceptance and respect, and her reading choices were often on the topic of slavery. She sought out books in the classroom and in the library on the Underground Railroad and Harriet Tubman. Her mother spoke to me of her deep interest and willingness to sit and listen while they read adult descriptions of life on the plantations. Her intense reaction to a *National Geographic* article complete with photographs of buildings with signs advertising slave auctions displayed an intellectual seriousness usually manifested at a much later time in learning, if at all. I was impressed and excited by her interest. The day she first saw the *National Geographic* article, Elissa and two friends started a very ambitious undertaking of trying to copy a painting shown in the article. The painting depicted slaves—adults and children—picking cotton in the fields. This project they planned provided them with an extended opportunity to study the painting and deepen their understanding of the life of Emily—our character-slave from *Next Stop Freedom* (Hoobler and Hoobler 1991).

Given a classroom where reflection, choice, and trust are valued, where the teacher respects the children's own styles and interests, where the teacher respects his or her own learning and shares that excitement with the children, children and teacher can generate a curriculum from the natural questions of the group. This curriculum can be relevant, authentic, and responsive to the needs of the group. I have learned from experience that second graders can learn about colonial times, slavery, and the Industrial Revolution in a meaningful way. They can relate to life during any time period, through the lives of other children—the characters in historical fiction.

Young Children's Reality

I know first graders at my school who, in preparation for a study of Japanese culture, were making passports for an imaginary trip to Japan and requested that their parents take them to the airport on the eve of the trip because they believed they were really going to Japan. As teachers we must have a clear understanding of the developmental expectations for children in our classrooms, individually and as a group. I don't believe we should pass up exciting content or exciting contexts for learning because children might not understand all concepts of time, place, and space. We do have an obligation to present people from their own points of view, and this is especially true when studying other cultures from the past. We must show the development of past cultures up through today, and dissolve stereotypes and generalizations such as "All Africans live in huts" and "All Eskimos live in igloos." Simulation so real that six-year-olds believed they were really going to Japan is far less worrisome than social studies taught through stereotypes.

Generating a Curriculum: Connecting the Past, Present, and Future

Much of what happened in my classroom each day—topics for writing and study groups, books for reading, projects for choice—was generated from read-aloud stories at meeting time. There was no attempt to begin or end units of study. The children cycled back as questions were raised and understanding deepened. Comparisons and references to times past were frequent. We began the year by talking about Columbus and the complexities of new understandings of that time. At Thanksgiving we measured and marked out a mock Mayflower ship, gathered the approximately correct number of people, and ate common crackers and beef jerky in the space. We talked about how the number of school days from the beginning of the school year to Thanksgiving was approximately the number of days the Pilgrims were on the Mayflower. The hardships the Pilgrims experienced on the Mayflower began to seem real. We invited the other second grades to make stone soup with us and to feast together after our Mayflower voyage.

One year, during choice/project time, children drew Underground Railroad maps. Students began making complex mazes as an outgrowth of these maps. Later on in the year when we studied mapping, they had a basis for understanding representational mapping. However, as making the mazes became a popular activity, I questioned to myself, Should I let this grow? Is this educationally sound? Is this connected to slavery? Does it matter? My instincts told me to let the mazes continue. Ben, the child who started the mazes, was really excited about creating them. He was invested in a way I hadn't seen before. His enthusiasm was contagious. Kids were making mazes at home with their families and bringing them in. The designs were revamped and reworked as children self-assessed, tried them out on each other, and decided they were too easy or too hard. This application of feedback, directly affecting design, was very exciting. There was real work going on for a particular clientele, or, as we say in regard to writing, a real audience.

The mazes led to games complete with game boards, playing pieces, directions, and boxes to contain it all. Students created most games with a partner. A couple of children preferred to work alone, and there was one threesome. This was, from my point of view, the most creative project of the year and also a high point for the children. They actually talked about selling their games to make money for their financially troubled school system. If you followed the sprouting and growth of the ideas and activities, you could see that surprisingly enough, the idea to make games came out of mazes—which came from maps made in an attempt to understand the Underground Railroad—which came from projects on the Underground Railroad—which came out of studying slavery.

This happened, I believe, because I allowed myself to trust the children's interests to guide us. I appreciate that this is very difficult to do when we are feeling the pressure of the prescribed curriculum. However, I recommend trusting the natural learning model. This scenario is one I could not have anticipated and one I could not have preplanned. Yes, I think it can be replicated, and I'll definitely make games again. However, nothing in the classroom is as authentic or as rewarding as that which springs forth naturally.

Making Connections: Mill Life

The study of the Industrial Revolution provided opportunities for social studies and science integration. We reflected back on our visit to Longfellow's Wayside Inn, where we had seen a grist mill. The children remembered the gears and waterwheel. It had been in operation grinding corn when we were there. Interest piqued around the workings of the mill and the relationship of mills to the Industrial Revolution.

Hannah, our mill girl's sister from the book *Hannah's Fancy Notions* (Ross 1992) was left in charge at home when Rebecca, the central character, traveled by stage coach to Lowell, Massachusetts (less than fifteen miles from our school) to work in the mills. Geography was naturally integrated as we followed the travels of each of our characters. This one was close to home, which added an element of reality for the children. There was much local geography to talk and learn about in relation to the physical location of mills near water and the relationship of the land to people's lives. We took a bus trip around Acton with a fifth-grade class and their teacher, Nancy Joslin, an expert on Acton history. There we visited sites of old mills and factories. Gun powder, barrels, pencils, and cheese were all made in Acton during this period.

Hannah and Rebecca's situation touched the children's sense of fairness, unconditional family love, and responsibilities of individuals (even children) toward those they love. Our class meeting talk was enriched with expressions of understanding, appreciation, and sympathy. As we discussed how Hannah and her sisters had accepted their Papa's sense of sadness and his inability to motivate himself to work, Adam, in a most unusual and very sensitive demonstration of intrapersonal skills (Gardner 1983) got right to the point and said that this was a "heart warming moment." He recognized that the children loved their father and understood his despair over their mother's death, and forgave him for the inconveniences it caused them financially and emotionally.

In one of the class plays about mill girls, the actors stood at sewing machines. They complained of the heat, illness, and the boss's angry manner. They shared feelings of being lonesome and of wanting to go home, but each had a clear sense that their families needed them to work. I was interested and impressed by the students' ability to write an informative script based on accurate details, deliver their lines with appropriate emotion, and cleverly plan the logistics of several scene and set changes (see Figure 3–6).

In order to assist children in their connections with and under-standings of Hannah and Rebecca's lives (including working conditions), my student teacher led the children in a brainstorming session to deter-mine what they already knew and what they wanted to know. From the list of what they wanted to know, they formulated a questionnaire to survey their parents about their own jobs (see Figure 3–7). The re-sponses made Rebecca's situation at the mill seem very extreme, which, of course, it was. There were many opportunities to use real math in understanding the data yielded by the job survey. Returning to the story, the children were motivated to understand money and gained the beginnings of understanding of multiplication and division as they examined the amount of money Rebecca earned each hour, day, week, month. Understanding the cost-of-living comparisons, the cost of rent at the boarding house, of hats, bandboxes, and transportation were of great interest to the children.

The children were applying factual content to their projects—for instance, that factories and mills were built near water sources. Understanding wheels was important to understanding mills. A bread factory was constructed using firsthand knowledge from a field trip to the Wonderbread factory in Natick, Massachusetts. Our science study of gears was real because of our visits to the grist mill and factory. A discussion of gears led to a discussion of bicycles and then an idea—to take apart a bike. At the workbench, before taking the bike apart, children drew accurate scientific drawings of the bike and labeled all the parts. As they took it apart, parts were carefully organized for the next step. Putting the bike back together certainly increased everyone's understanding of its complexities.

Conclusion

Often children confused time periods and continents while integrating ideas naturally. They were, after all, still second graders grappling with

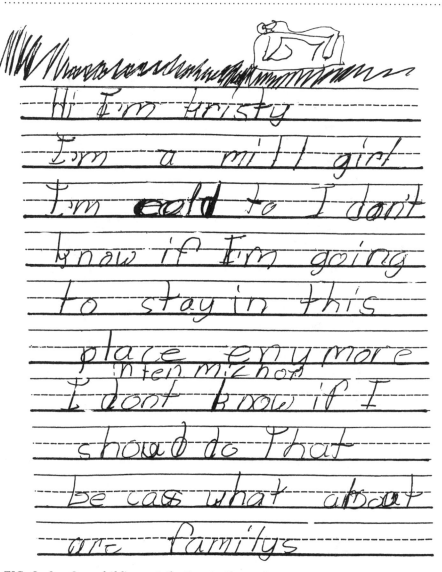

FIG. 3–6   One child's contribution to the script

complex ideas, and some of the concepts of time and space were not fully understood. However, the understandings of man's inhumanity to man and the strength of the human spirit were clearly theirs. As they add to their repertoire of experiences with American history, their understandings of time—of what happened when—will deepen and so will their knowledge of geography. Examples of the children's sensitivity

QUESTIONS TO ASK A PARENT OR A FRIEND WHO WORKS

1 **WHAT TYPE OF OCCUPATION DO YOU DO?** ✓

work with lones.
In a Bank.

2 **HOW MANY HOURS DO YOU USUALLY WORK PER DAY?** ✓

nine hours a day.

3 **WHAT DOES THE BUILDING YOU WORK IN LOOK LIKE?** ✓

Brick bilding, three floors, lots of windows, elervater, big parking lot.

4 **DO YOU GET A LUNCH BREAK?   IF YES, FOR HOW LONG?** ✓

yes! 30 minutes.

5 **DOES IT HAVE HEAT AND AIR CONDITIONING?** ✓

yes it does.

6 **DO YOU GET TIME OFF FOR SICK DAYS OR VACATION?** ✓

no he does not

7 **DO YOU HAVE A CHAIR TO SIT DOWN IN?** ✓

yes!

8 **WHAT TIME TO YOU HAVE TO BE AT WORK IN THE MORNING?** ✓

eight-o-clock in the morning.

FIG. 3–7   Job survey

to our historical characters and to each other were apparent in daily living in the classroom. Children frequently spoke of their own or of someone else's feelings in reference to a situation under discussion. They were quick to identify with the characters in our books. Problems affecting people of various times in the past were thought, talked, and written about, and played out. Their respect for humankind, each other included, was growing and real.

"In Fairness to All" and "Francen the Flamingo" are both stories generated by children in response to and while living in an environment that encouraged responsibility for making other people feel comfortable. The first is a story about race relations in which Ali, a member of the class, demonstrates a level of sophistication most unusual for her age. The second is a story within a story presenting two morals: not to brag, and the importance and value of forgiveness in friendship. To me this is social studies at its finest.

The literature we read as a class provided us with shared experiences through the lives of the characters. The artifacts in and out of the cabin added tangible realism to our studies of the past. Together we enriched our understandings of the past, of ourselves, and of each other. With this classroom structure, children had the power to generate curriculum projects and the supports to help them in designing their own learning. They were choosing the aspects of learning that were most important to them. Each event, project, discussion, story, and character became something else with which to connect. The children saw their learning as a natural outgrowth of living in the classroom together.

As for Assessment

In my classroom, children's work—math diaries, writing, and projects—stayed in the classroom and were readily available for affirmation, reflection, and sharing with and by the teacher, parents, classmates, and visitors. Selected pieces were chosen to become part of the students' portfolios, which will follow them throughout their elementary school years. Parent-teacher conferences were held in the fall and in the spring. Discussion during these conferences centered around the students artifacts. In March, the children had conferences with their enthusiastic and appreciative parents and shared their works-in-process and completed efforts with great pride. Learning was validated by and for the children. The children could speak eloquently about their progress and had clear understandings of their growth. They also had specific goals for future growth. My role in this process was to guide children in reflecting on their learning and to assist them in preparing and organizing for the conference. Children wrote to parents as part of their reflection and preparation (see Figure 3–8). They outlined a list of things they wanted to be sure to share with their parents (see Figure 3–9). Parents wrote to their children during the conference. Children wrote again after the

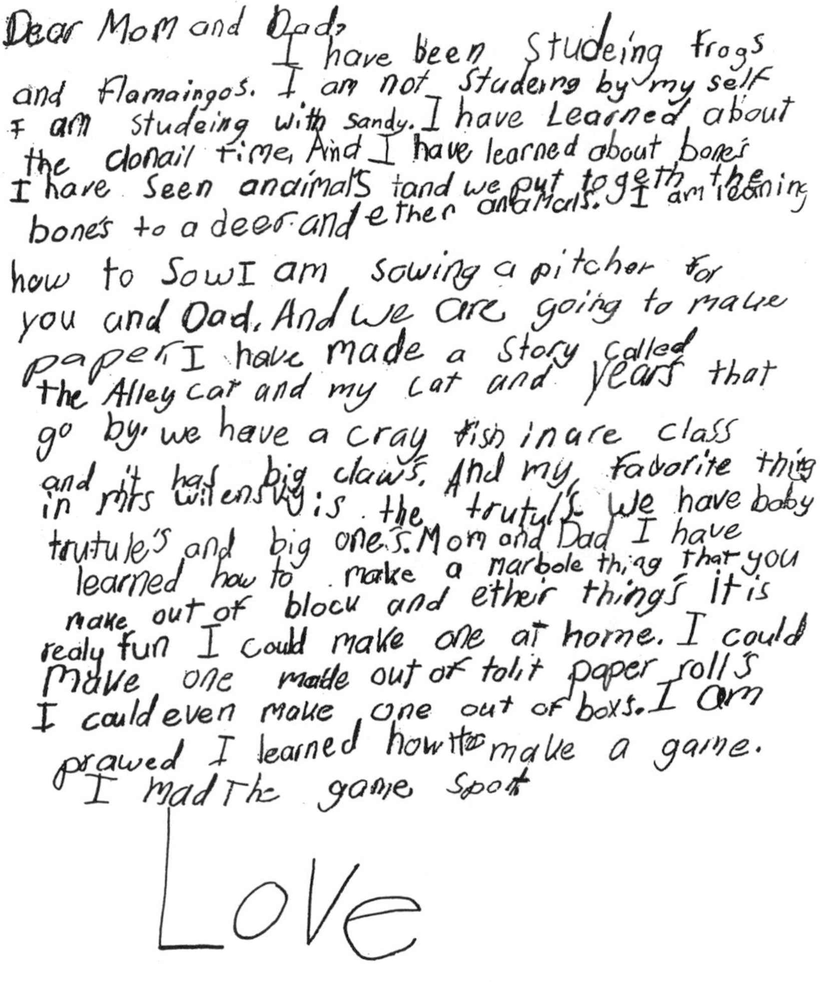

Dear Mom and Dad,
I have been studeing frogs
and flamaingos. I am not studeing by my self
I am studeing with sandy. I have learned about
the clonail time, And I have learned about bones
I have seen andimals tand we put togeth the
bones to a deer and ether animals. I am leaning
how to SowI am sowing a pitcher for
you and Dad. And we are going to make
paper I have made a story called
the Alley cat and my cat and years that
go by. we have a cray fish in are class
and it has big claws. And my favorite thing
in rits wilensky is the trutyls We have baby
trutule's and big one.s Mom and Dad I have
learned how to make a marbole thing that you
make out of block and ether things It is
realy fun I could make one at home. I could
make one made out of tolit paper rolls
I could even make one out of boxs. I am
prawed I learned how to make a game.
I madrhe game spoot

Love

FIG. 3–8   Letter to parent

conference about their feelings about the conference (see Figure 3–10).
At the end of the year, parents filled out a questionnaire about the
conference and their child's learning that year (see Figure 3–11). Ideas
used in planning this procedure came from *Evaluating Literacy* (Anthony, Johnson, Michelson, and Preece 1991).

Social Studies and Literacy in the Second Grade

.... 51

What I have learned in Second Grade:

writing: Penny and the Snowmian ✓

Journals - 2 Journel Pages ✓

Story writing - longer storys ✓

Punctuation - Peroids, Comias, cotashon marks ✓

words - longer words ✓

Spelling - more sounds ✓

reading: Chapter books ✓

math: Math with Deins blocks

⊕ addition - add to 1000 ✓

⊖ Subtraction - take away from 1000 ✓

⊗ times - every thing times o is the other number ✓

$ money - Dimes, Nickels, Pennies, quarters, Dollars.

Science

animals - rabbits.

machines - factorys, mills.

Social studies

- past - Knickers, girls wore bng skirts
  Quilt - making Pictures
      time line - drawing Pictures and putting dates
      Slavery - black people were slaves   below
  industreal regilution   them

FIG. 3–9   *Student list for letter to parent*

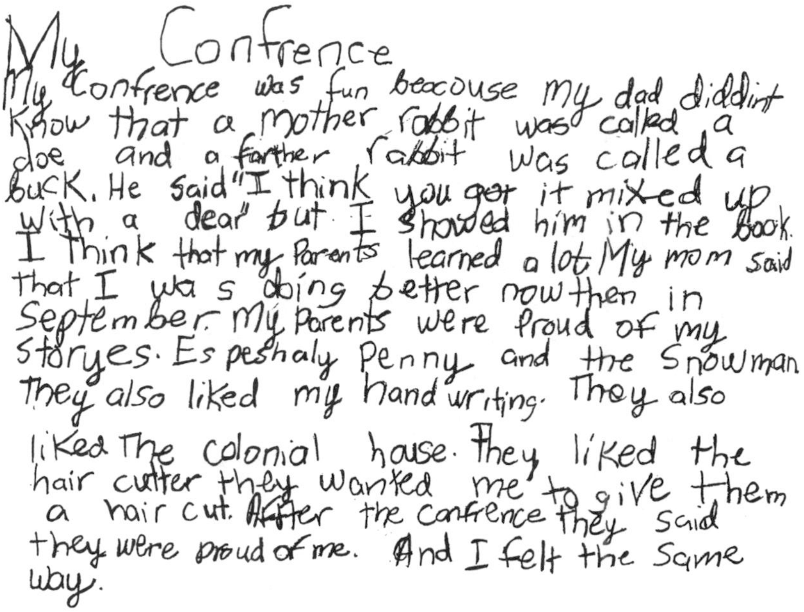

My Confrence

My Confrence was fun beacouse my dad diddint know that a mother rabbit was called a doe and a farther rabbit was called a buck. He said "I think you get it mixed up with a dear" but I showed him in the book. I think that my Parents learned a lot My mom said that I was doing better now then in September. My Parents were proud of my storyes. Es peshaly Penny and the Snowman. They also liked my hand writing. They also

liked The colonial house. They liked the hair cutter they wanted me to give them a hair cut. After the confrence they said they were proud of me. And I felt the Same way.

FIG. 3–10   *Conference summary*

1 **Is your child's learning in second grade as you hoped and anticipated?**

Yes, Maria has enjoyed second grade more than other grades previously experienced. You create an academic, yet stimulating and comfortable environment for the children and I feel a lot of learning has been going on throughout the year in an enjoyable way for bringing out each childs individual strengths

2. **Is your child's social development progressing as you hoped and anticipated?**

I didn't even mention cooperative learning that was constantly going on within the classroom!

Yes. I feel that Maria, through conversation, experienced a great deal of social development in several different ways. Within the classroom, reading buddies (both older and younger than herself and through student teachers.) I did not anticipate her social development to be as great as it has been. She enjoys people very much and this was fostered because of you (thanks.

3. **Did you find the conference with your child demonstrated her/his learning in a clear way that you could appreciate?** Yes, I also felt that she was very pleased with what she was accomplishing in "her" classroom. I think it gave her a sense of "power" and control over what was said and she was able to show us "what "she" thought was important to her. She had a good time sharing a part of her life that we don't get to see.

4. **What specific areas of growth were most obvious to you through this student-led conference procedure? Consider all areas of development: social, cognitive-academic, emotional. Please be as specific as you can.** She was able to lead the conference w/ ease. She was confident of her accomplishments and proud of her work. (She did not want to forget to share one thing with us.) We heard it all! I thought it was great. Thank you for giving up your time on a Sunday to accomodate both parents.

5: **Do you have any concerns at this time? Please explain.** My only concern is for next year. I would like to keep her motivation as it stands today. High. She enjoys school and she makes me feel that its to her, like a home away from home. She has learned a lot this year in many subject areas. She also has had fun doing it.

It takes a special type of "person-teacher" to foster this type of learning environment and I thank you for giving Maria a school year that she will probably always look back on with very fond memories. (And you going down the hill on the tray!)

FIG. 3–11   *Parent questionnaire*

References

Anthony, Robert, Terry Johnson, Norma Michelson, and Alison Preece. 1991. *Evaluating Literacy*. Portsmouth, NH: Heinemann.

Dahl, Roald. 1984. *Charlie and the Chocolate Factory*. New York: Bantam.

Dalgliesh, Alice. 1987. *The Courage of Sarah Noble*. New York: MacMillan.

Duckworth, Eleanor. 1987. *The Having of Wonderful Ideas and Other Essays on Teaching and Learning*. New York: Teachers College Press.

Gardner, Howard. 1983. *Frames of Mind: The Theory of Multiple Intelligences*. New York: Basic.

Gross, Virginia. 1992. *It's Only Goodbye*. New York: Puffin.

Hoobler, Dorothy, and Thomas Hoobler. 1991. *Next Stop Freedom: The Story of a Slave Girl*. New York: Silver Burdett.

Kudlinski, Kathleen. 1992. *Hero over Here: A Story of World War I*. New York: Puffin.

MacLachlan, Patricia. 1987. *Sarah, Plain and Tall*. New York: Harper Collins.

Oneal, Zibby. 1990. *A Long Way to Go*. New York: Viking.

Ross, Pat. 1992. *Hannah's Fancy Notions: A Story of Industrial New England*. New York: Puffin.

Pat Reflects—

When I read Sandra's account of her classroom explorations, I feel that I see the very best of literature and social studies paired together. Using historical fiction as a bridge to understanding the past is something I really only associated with upper grades and adults until I talked to whole language primary teachers and saw the powerful uses of literature in history for young children. I don't know why I didn't make the connection.

When I taught first and second grade myself, a long time ago, I was still struggling to use the basal reader and the reading kits that were current at the time. It wasn't until I taught third grade that I broke through into real literature, and then I wasn't very focused on social studies. My students and I read and read, usually books that they chose. We talked about the events, times, and peoples of those books but I never made the link to social studies, probably because of limitations in my own thinking. My notion of social studies in those days was to discuss the meaning of the pledge of allegiance and maybe to take a field trip in the spring.

But as Sandra says, our goals with children of all ages must be to help them "see themselves as a part of history" and "to bring the children into the context of the time period they are studying." And authentic historical fiction provides the very best vehicle for children of all ages. Through those shared experiences, children are able to, in Dorothy Heathcote's words, "walk in the times."

As in Bobbi's chapter, Sandra writes of developing "structures" through which she and her students could explore communities in American History. Some of these structures were concrete, such as the cabin she and her students maintained throughout the study, but some were learning structures. These learning structures were more than procedures, more than classroom routines, and much more than mere activities. Rather, they were an integral way of living and exploring together in the classroom, tying together curricular, social, academic, and behavioral strands of acting and thinking. These learning structures were visible as patterns of movement and interaction, equity and dynamics. A guest would see classroom participants "going about the business of the day," rather than responding to a list of teacher directions on the board. This dynamic interaction was experienced by the students and teacher as the work of the classroom, with all participants purposeful and intent. This is what Sandra calls "a daily wealth of shared and meaningful experiences" from which the classwork and curriculum grew. This daily wealth and the activity that accompanies it were the result of children and adults fully engaged in learning with everyone knowing what there was to be done and actively and meaningfully setting about to do it. As Sandra puts it, "nothing in the classroom is as authentic or as rewarding as that which springs forth naturally."

Judy Blatt loves drama—her students know that before they enter her third grade. Every year she writes original plays for her students, based on what they're learning in the classroom. Every simulation eventually winds up as a play, which serves as a culminating activity for that unit. Her third graders love performing in the plays, and the rest of the students, parents, and staff that make up the school community enjoy watching them sing, dance, and act. Judy says that doing this work is about "finding the best in yourself and in the kids."

Judy grew up in New York City during what she calls "The Golden Age of Musicals," many of which she attended with her dad. A high school drama course was a favorite, and she says she can remember every play she was ever in. Inspired by her own powerful memories, Judy believes that plays are really important in the lives of children, and she continues to enjoy every aspect of make-believe.

During Judy's first year of teaching in New York City's South Bronx, she was told that every class had to do a play. She read through a few children's plays, and was dismayed to discover that each featured just a handful of children in large parts, with the rest of the class relegated to flower or tree status. Judy felt that every child should be a star. She wrote her own play, with a speaking role for each of her thirty-six students.

Teacher and students enjoyed the experience, and Judy continued to create plays for the students at Haynes Elementary School in Sudbury, Massachusetts, where she has now taught for twenty-two years. She says her purpose is not to turn third graders into actors and actresses, but instead to use the plays as a learning vehicle for science and social studies. In addition, plays help children gain confidence, think creatively, and learn to speak more clearly. Judy adds that working on a play together is fun for everyone and gives a class a wonderful esprit de corps.

Judy acknowledges that some teachers may not have the time or inclination to produce an original play, and she reminds us that all of her simulations can be done very successfully without doing a play. For those who decide to give it a go, Judy feels it's important to make sure the whole class participates in writing the play. She always starts out her plays with a script, but encourages students to change their parts as needed. Sometimes parts have even been changed during a performance, to Judy's surprise, such as the time one of the characters unexpectedly produced powder to use for fingerprinting. Judy and her students work to tailor the parts to the kids. Actors do memorize lines, but retain the freedom to change them.

Judy has directed performances for casts of varied sizes, including a single class, all the classes in one grade, and the whole school. Each year on the first day of school, to show how easy it is, she has her class write a simple script together. Each child contributes one line, and sometimes they perform this play for other classes. Another annual event is the Martin Luther King play, which Judy adapts each year to involve every student in her school. In recent years, Judy's plays have taken on an added dimension with the addition of original music written by her colleague, music teacher Marty Schneider. She hopes this collaboration will continue.

Putting on plays does take time, Judy says. But if you believe in their value, then the time you take is worth it.

CHAPTER FOUR

Simulations in the Third Grade

Judy Blatt

"I see you're practicing for a play," a visitor exclaimed as he walked into my third-grade classroom. No, we weren't, but his mistake was understandable. The children were dressed in strange and unusual outfits. Some were wearing straw hats, others wore wigs, shawls, large jackets, and long skirts. It certainly looked like a dress rehearsal—but it wasn't. Our visitor actually arrived in the middle of a science lesson about the solar system.

If the visitor had stayed longer he would have noticed that each child wore a name tag with a fictitious name and that the name "Dr. J. B." was taped to my lab coat. Had he listened, he would have heard a serious discussion about the atmosphere on the planet Jupiter. Had he known me, he would have recognized that the rather brisk manner of speaking I had adopted—as Dr. J. B.—was not my normal mode of addressing the class.

The children and I were all role-playing, but we weren't practicing for a play. Instead, we were acting out a simulation of a group of scientists meeting to plan a trip into space. We were sharing knowledge gleaned from our research. Yes, we were indeed studying the solar system, and we needed to learn as much as possible to design spaceships for exploring the universe.

Information about the moon becomes more meaningful to a child if he or she is planning to make a trip to the earth's satellite with friends. When everyone around a student, including the teacher, is immersed in this simulation, it's easy to get caught up in the situation as well. Reading and writing about the solar system becomes charged with an energy, a need to know, so that everyone can participate in the group's project.

Children love to dress up and pretend to be different people in a make-believe situation. That's why simulations work so well. But in the last few years I made a discovery about myself: I also enjoy make-believe.

JUDY BLATT

60 $\cdots\cdots\cdots\cdots\cdots\cdots\cdots\cdots\cdots\cdots\cdots\cdots\cdots\cdots\cdots\cdots\cdots\cdots\cdots\cdots\cdots\cdots\cdots$

I love creating the situations and then playing a part and becoming involved in the story that unfolds. Where else would I have the opportunity to be the chairman of the board of a society of mammal lovers, a detective with Scotland Yard, or the CEO of an advertising company? (I give myself very important roles.) I don't underestimate the importance of my enjoyment. As a teacher who has been around for a long time, I can see the pitfalls of the easy route, the same old routines. Children are much more apt to be motivated by a teacher who is having fun. Simulations are one of the paths I take to keep those bubbles of anticipation strong as I drive to school each morning. And the situations you can dream up are infinite. You are limited only by your imagination.

I have discovered six elements that contribute to the success of my simulations. To begin, you need to think of an idea that you find believable. You must be able to carry off your role with a straight face. If you start laughing because you think you have created a ridiculous situation, it won't work. If you take the situation and the problem seriously, the children will too. The situation you have created isn't nearly as important as the way you approach it, because if it doesn't work out the way you planned, you can always alter your scenerio. Since you created it, you are free to change its direction. However, once the children get involved, simulations have a way of developing a life of their own.

The second element is written resources. You can set up the simulation and have the entire class enthralled by the roles they are going to play, but if they lack resources for them to learn on their own, your simulation will die an early death. So before you begin, you must try to acquire as many books as possible on the subject your class is studying. You will need to be sure that information is in books written at the students' level and that there are enough books for everyone. I am fortunate that buying books for theme studies is a high priority for Chet Delani, the principal of my school.

The third key component is people. When my children were involved in the mystery simulation, two of our most interesting guests were a private detective and a state trooper from the state crime lab. The veterinarian who came to our class was a wonderful role model for the "veterinarians" in our Mammal Society. My colleagues have also been invaluable. Our school has a music teacher who creates original songs, an art teacher who dreams up projects for every theme, a secretary who loves to dress up, a special needs teacher who doubles as an actress, and my "partner in crime" from the adjoining classroom, who has worked with me on the mystery simulation for many years. If you look around your school, I'm sure you will find many talented people happy to play a part in your simulations, too.

The fourth component consists of blank books. The books are used for keeping notes, writing letters, stories, jingles, raps, poetry, songs, or dialogue. Since the children use the same book for a number of different theme studies, I have them call it "The Adventure Book." The students start a new section every time they begin to study a new theme.

The fifth element, costumes, is not an essential part of a simulation, but most children feel they do a better job of role-playing when they are dressed for the part. Some children don't care to don a costume, and that's OK, too. A box of old clothing in the classroom is great not only for simulations but for acting out skits or plays.

I have a costume closet in my classroom. Teachers and parents have contributed old clothes and costumes over the years. I have some wonderful props, too. Telephones are useful, and last year I borrowed a gavel from one of my children's parents to call meetings of the Mammal Society of America to order. I have a Greek helmet, crutches, and even a pair of wings from a Halloween bird costume.

When we are in the middle of a simulation, children keep their costumes in their desks, hanging from the back of their chairs, or in a shoe box. However, I only let the children wear them during that part of the day when we are living the simulation, so that the activities seem more special. Throughout the day the children move in and out of simulations easily.

I have found that name tags are a good idea, too. During simulations, it is easier for me to keep track of the children's "names" if they write them on an index card and tape the cards to their clothing. Some of the children prefer using their own names, and I respect their wishes.

Finally, you must listen to the children and listen carefully. This is the most important element of a successful simulation and is a fundamental part of all good teaching. Actively solicit their input with pointed questions, initiate discussions on matters large and small, and encourage voting when appropriate. If you are stumped for solutions, ask the children to help. When a simulation is not going well, ask the children why there is a problem and if they can suggest new strategies. You may not like their answers, but you do need to see their point of view. They need to know that their education is a joint venture for teacher and students. They need to be aware that their input is important to you.

A response journal is an excellent tool for gathering opinions and suggestions. My children and I frequently communicate with each other in this fashion. They call the journal the "Communicator Book" to distinguish it from the "Adventure Book." Whenever possible, I incorporate their ideas into my plans and acknowledge the children who are responsible for the suggestions.

I divide simulations into three types. I call the first "Facilitated Families." When my class studies ancient Greece, I divide them into ancient Greek "families" living the daily life of people of that time and place. I act as a facilitator rather than as a resident of their world. This model could be adapted for the study of any culture.

In the second, called "Chairman of the Board," I am chairman or president of the group. I call meetings, read letters I have written, and play a dominant role. I used this model for the studies of Massachusetts, Mammals, and the Solar System.

The third category is "Mystery." It is a creative problem-solving simulation that my class and a fourth-grade class engage in every other year. The children become detectives and figure out who committed a murder and a robbery.

For the remainder of this chapter I will discuss these three kinds of simulations. For each type of simulation, I describe my own experiences with my classes. You may wish to adapt them to suit your own teaching style, your curriculum requirements, your school environment, and the interests of your students.

Ancient Greece

In preparation for the study of ancient Greece, I divide my class into groups of three, four, and five. Four is the ideal number. Much thought must be given to the makeup of the groups, because the groups become families and it is important for the families to stay constant. This simulation works best when the members of the families get along well. Why make life harder than it needs to be by grouping together children who don't see eye-to-eye on anything? The study could go on for months, and that's a long time to play referee.

First, we place the desks in clusters so the children can sit with their families. Then I give each child a list of common Greek names and a copy of the Greek alphabet. For the first assignment, each child must choose a Greek name and age. I have a rule that no child may be younger than eight. Children who choose the baby role don't do productive work.

Next, the family must decide how they are all related to each other. We have brothers and sisters, mothers and fathers, aunts and uncles. It's not surprising that third graders don't choose to take the roles of married couples. Each family then picks a Greek letter for a family name, so we have the Alpha family, the Beta family, and the Sigma family. Last year we also had the Chrysoulouros family, because Elli Chrysoulouros's group argued successfully that Elli had a Greek name and that it was more authentic than a Greek letter. The children write their new names on cards to keep on their desks. A sign with the family name hanging above each family is a good idea, too, if you have a place to hang the signs, because it's not always easy to remember which family is Zeta and which is Delta.

Children take the proceedings very seriously and the arguments over family names and relationships can get very hot until it is all sorted out. Once every child has a new identity and a place within a family, I tell them to take out their Adventure Books, title the new section "My Diary," and write their Greek names on that page.

The purpose of the first entry is to identify the author of the diary and to give a brief description of the family. Every entry is dated, which always provokes an interesting discussion about how you date entries when you are writing in ancient times. How can you write B.C. if it is before the time of Christ? Last year we finally agreed to write the day of the week (Monday, Tuesday, etc.) because it made the most sense to us.

I try to have the children use their diaries as much as possible. At first it is hard for children to write with the voice of a resident of ancient Greece, but it soon becomes second nature to them. In fact, some children still use their Greek names for an assignment weeks after we stop studying about ancient Greece.

Now that the children have names and families, all they need to make them feel they belong in ancient Athens are homes. After examining pictures of ancient Greek homes and discussing the reasons for the similarities to and differences from their own homes, they are ready to create floor plans of their ancient Greek family homes. Each family works together and plans its own home. Each home must contain sleeping quarters for every child in the group, as well as some basic elements of a typical ancient Greek home. I love listening to the discussions that evolve. The size and contents of each room become extremely important, and the child who forgets and wants a TV in his room quickly has his memory jogged into ancient times by his "brothers" or "sisters."

Pillowcases make wonderful tunics. It's very easy to cut out openings for the head and arms, and the children love to decorate them with magic markers. The ancient Greeks wore colorful tunics, so they don't have to be white. Now the theme study can begin in earnest, and all the books my school owns on ancient Greece are put to good use. The children read, and we discuss what they have read. Then they weave the factual information into the diary accounts of their daily lives.

I organize the study by subject. If we read about the theater, every child has to write a diary entry about his or her family and the theater. Cooperative learning is essential when children have to write about family activities—how can John ("Dimitri") write about what Sally ("Aunt Kara") was doing without asking her? Each diary entry must be unique, but the information about the family should agree, and the facts about ancient Greece must be accurate. I do insist on facts. I usually set the minumum number of facts per entry at six. This is the type of entry children write, with at least six facts:

Dear Diary,
Yesterday my whole family went to the theater. My Aunt Kara woke us up at the crack of dawn so we could get there early and get good seats. Too bad everyone in Athens had the same idea. We sat so far away from the stage I was afraid I wouldn't be able to see and naturally Dimitri started to complain. But we had no problems because the actors wore masks and elevated shoes. Poor Thea, how she would love to be down there with the actors but only boys are permitted to act in the plays. After awhile I got tired of sitting on the stone seat out in the hot sun and I was so glad Thea brought the pillows.

Another facet of the ancient Greek study in my class is Greek mythology. The children read numerous Greek myths, discuss them, and then write stories in their journals based on the themes of the myths. This writing must be incorporated into the simulation too.

A diary entry about Pandora might begin, "Last night my father read the story of Pandora to me. Pandora reminds me of my Cousin Georgi. Cousin Georgi is always getting into trouble because he is so curious . . ." Then the author of that entry might go on to relate just what Cousin Georgi did that earned him a reputation for curiosity. Again, all facts of daily life would have to be checked. Each child should be ready to show the source of his or her information.

When it's time to put an end to the study of ancient Greece, it's fun to finish in a dramatic way. The last entry is written in the middle of a terrible earthquake and the children have their writing slip off the page in the middle of a sentence. Then they write an epilogue, which is supposed to have been written by the person who found the diary this year.

The study of ancient Greece in my classroom has taken different paths. Some years each family has chosen one special topic and studied it in depth. These children wrote more detailed entries accompanied by illustrations and put up their own family bulletin board displays, complete with the portraits of each member of the family and the layout of their homes. One year the children read and acted out entries from their diaries on the stage at a school meeting. Other years we've had ancient Greek newspapers, plays, and Greek feasts.

The children point the way and tell me what they want to know. They learn more because the daily life of a group of people who lived thousands of years ago relates in a very special way to the lives of these students in my room.

Massachusetts

Some themes naturally lend themselves to involvement and drama, but I never found this to be so with the study of Massachusetts. It always seemed to be the hump I had to climb over before I could get on with the more interesting third-grade topics like simple machines and mammals. However, it was part of the required third-grade social studies curriculum, so I had no choice but to keep on teaching it. Then one day I thought of turning my class into an advertising agency. If the state Chamber of Commerce hired my ad agency to attract tourists to Massachusetts, then the members of the firm would have to learn about the state before they could persuade others to visit. It certainly seemed worth a try. After a brief discussion with my class, I realized that they knew enough about advertising for me to get started with the simulation. I owe a debt of thanks to Prilly Sanville. I borrowed freely from her techniques for the introduction. "I'm going to leave the class for just a few minutes, and when I return we are going to create an imaginary situation," I began. "We will pretend to be meeting in the boardroom of an advertising company in New York City. You will all be adults, members of the firm called Pinkle, Finkle, and Twinkle, and I am going to be president of the company. You may call me JB. If you feel that being part of this advertising company is too difficult to do, please just sit quietly and observe us." (I have set up many simulations in a similar fashion since then and never once have I had a child who didn't want to get into the act.)

When I returned a few minutes later I was wearing a jacket and hat and I carried a briefcase. "I'm sorry I'm late," I said breathlessly, "but you want to know why I called this meeting, so I won't waste any time. I received an important letter in the mail and I can't wait to read it to you."

At this point I pulled a letter I had written the night before out of an envelope and began to read dramatically:

To the Members of the Advertising Firm of Pinkle, Finkle, and Twinkle:

We are writing to you because the state of Massachusetts is in trouble. The job situation is bad and our reputation is not what it used to be. Tourists are staying away. We need to bring the tourists back. That is why we would like to hire your company to mount an advertising campaign to attract people and convince them to visit our state. We know it seems unusual to hire a New York firm but we felt you could look at our state with fresh eyes, and we heard you were the best. We hope to hear from you soon. Are you interested in the job?

Sincerely,

Joe Smith, Massachusetts Chamber of Commerce

My roomful of young executives voted to take on the job, and we were on our way. The title of this section of the Adventure Book was the "Massachusetts Advertising Campaign." The first entry in that section was a letter to Joe Smith. Each child not only accepted the job in that letter, but also outlined some future plans and signed the letter with her or his new name. All ideas for the campaign were jotted down in the book. Children also used the book for their notes, lists, letters, jingles, and raps. In addition, they made up board games and a Massachusetts alphabet book for children.

The children did the same research my classes had done in previous years. Other classes had learned about famous people and famous places and so did they. Earlier classes had studied history and geography, learned about natural resources and industry, and so did they. But the children had a different point of view this time and a different goal. As young advertising executives, they functioned as a team with a job to do. My challenge was to keep the simulation moving along and the children involved with the study. I made sure that letters from the Chamber of Commerce arrived from time to time. Joe Smith was always interested in progress reports and each letter called for a response. When it was time for the study to end, I wrote Joe's last letter, a thank-you for a job well done.

The following year I wanted to do a simulation again but I didn't want to repeat the same one, so I created the Medkovs. They were a poor Russian family who wanted to come to the United States to live. I was the chairman and the children were members of the Sudbury Outreach Committee, a committee formed to teach Boris, Maya, and their children Sasha, ten, and Vera, eight, about their new home. Of course the committee had to learn all about their state before they could help this family.

This simulation took an interesting turn when I added two new characters, Grandma and Grandpa Medkov. They wrote a heartrending letter in which they described their overwhelming desire to join Boris, Maya, and the two children in Sudbury. Of course the Sudbury Medkovs were poor and so was the Outreach Committee, so we invented a TV game called "The USA Game." Contestants would be quizzed on a different state each week. The Medkovs needed to become experts on Massachusetts so they could compete in the show. The winners would get $100,000, more than enough to bring Grandma and Grandpa to the United States.

The children enjoyed making up questions and answers about Massachusetts for the game. The simulation culminated in a play we put on for the entire school, with three families competing for the prize. Naturally the Medkovs (with heavy Russian accents) walked off with the $100,000, but everyone in the class felt like a winner when the audience cheered for the Medkov team.

This year the simulation involved a group of out-of-work actors and actresses trying to create commercials about Massachusetts that would bring them employment. I don't know what next year's Massachusetts simulation will be, but the one thing I am certain of is that it will be different from those I've done in the previous years.

Mystery

Imagine a classroom of third and fourth graders. Suddenly the door swings open. A woman in a trench coat enters. She has on Groucho Marx glasses and mustache. The children know it's their teacher (me), but before they have a chance to laugh, she speaks. "I have bad news for you. Charles Fahnsworth III is dead. I know it's a terrible shock to all of you. I'm sorry I have to be the one to tell you. He was poisoned last night at his estate. It was arsenic in his stew."

While I am speaking, the fourth-grade teacher, my friend and cohort, Mary Saltas, is giving out a form to each child. I continue in a solemn voice, "As Chief Inspector of Scotland Yard, I authorize you to fill out these forms. We must do so immediately."

The top half of the police report has already been completed, and the children read along as I read aloud from my copy.

Name of Victim: Charles Fahnsworth III
Address: The Fahnsworth Estate, Fahnsworth, England
Age: 40
Height: 5′ 11″
Weight: 180 lbs.
Hair Color: Black with some gray
Married: Yes
Occupation: Banker

The crime data on the bottom half of the form needs to be filled in, so I dictate that information while Mary copies it on the blackboard. The children become involved in the mechanics of writing. I move along quickly. There is no time for comments or questions.

Date of Death: May 6
Time: 7:00 P.M.
Place: Fahnsworth Estate—The Library
Cause of Death: Arsenic in Stew
Suspects: _____

When I come to the word *suspects*, I stop. We ask the children who might have killed this wealthy Englishman, and compile the list on the board. The children suggest the butler, the maid, his wife, his second wife, his nephew, the gardener, etc.

Then comes the zinger. I turn to face the class and look around slowly before I say, "You are the suspects. Someone in this room killed Charles Fahnsworth III, and we are going to find the culprit today."

Paper is distributed and the suspects are instructed to write a statement for Scotland Yard. Their first paragraph must tell who they are and what their relationship is to the deceased. The second paragraph should give a detailed description of their activities on May 6.

When the statements are complete, the children are instructed to read them aloud to each other in groups comprised of third and fourth graders. Each group is to choose the person who has written the most convincing statement and sounds the most like a genuine suspect.

The suspects (we usually wind up with about ten) get to pick costumes and then go out in the hall. I leave with the suspects, and Mary primes the rest of the children, who then become detectives. In the hall the children draw lots to pick the poisoner. It's the fastest and fairest way to find a culprit.

The suspects make signs to identify themselves so that when the detectives start their questioning they can call on the suspects by name. The suspects sit in front of the class and take turns reading their statements aloud. Some get into the spirit of the investigation easily and read their prepared statement as if they were really the butler or second wife; others are shy and take a while to warm up.

Then the fun begins. The detectives will find the murderer by questioning the suspects. They direct the questions to individual suspects, and the suspects have to make up answers. Both the suspects and detectives are challenged to use their wits. They must listen, and they must think fast. The children soon get caught up in this make-believe situation. Alibis begin to mesh into the web of a whole story. The imaginary Fahnsworth Estate soon has an east wing and a west wing. Charles Fahnsworth, a man who had many enemies, begins to develop a personality. Did the gardener change his story? If the cook was in the kitchen at 9:30, why didn't she see Charles Fahnsworth's nephew—who claimed he stopped in to grab a snack? The sleuths try to outdo each other quizzing the suspects and uncovering inconsistencies in their testimony.

When I decide the questioning has gone on long enough, each detective is invited to make an accusation—but it must be substantiated. The detectives often disagree among themselves. Finally a vote is called and quite often, but not always, the detectives choose the "real" murderer.

In order to keep the simulation fresh for us, Mary and I choose different victims each time. We prefer the rich and famous. One year we dispatched Lenora Lemora, a famous movie star of days gone by. She acquired great wealth and many "friends" as she traveled from obscurity to fame. Then there was Selina Sue, the glamorous star of the successful long-running soap opera "Magnolia Days." She was shot by a real bullet from a real gun someone substituted for the prop gun that should have been used on her final episode of the show.

The creative problem-solving simulation I described is just the introduction to a month of mystery activities Mary and I plan for our classes. During that month we pair each third grader with a fourth grader, and they become sleuths who attempt to solve a robbery committed at a school. The partners establish their identities by making business cards, filling out Police I.D. forms, drawing their own portraits, and creating full-page ads to attract business.

Detectives dress for the part. They may wear whatever they choose but all items must fit into a shoe box kept in their desks. An amazing amount of junk can be stuffed into one shoe box. Wigs, scarves, sunglasses, pipes, magnifying glasses, and hats help transform our children into private eyes. Now the detectives are ready for Madam X, the mystery lady. I put on a large hat and read the following letter with my back to the class:

To Whom It May Concern:

I saw your ad in the Boston GIobe. Something of great value has disappeared and I just don't know what to do. I am perplexed, puzzled, bewildered, and terribly upset that it could happen to me. If the public were to hear of this calamity I would be disgraced and ruined. I need your help desperately but only if you have the right qualifications.

If you are the suitable sleuth for this crime please reply in writing immediately. I need to know:
   1. How did you learn to be a detective?
   2. What important robberies have you solved?
   3. The names and telephone numbers of your clients.
   4. Do you charge by the hour or the case? How much?
   5. How long do you think it will take you to solve the crime?
Please send me one of your business cards.

Frantically,

Madam X

P.S. Please respond in your best cursive writing using paragraphs and complete sentences. Proofread for spelling errors.

The detectives respond to Madam X's letter (in their best cursive writing). Her next letter to them reveals that she is the principal of an elementary school called Kendall Lakes and that something of great value was stolen from the showcase in the lobby of her school the previous day at 10:00 A.M. She is positive it was an inside job, and the detectives must therefore be very discreet because a scandal would ensue if the news leaked to the public. The children are curious about the stolen object because the letter did not contain a description of it. Madam X didn't offer them a clue.

   Therefore, their first assignment is to decide on an appropriate object. The teams of detectives go to the library to search through encyclopedias and magazines for a valuable object. They read about gems, ancient artifacts, and antiques, and each team chooses a favorite. They are able to use their own school for all assignments because we tell them that the Kendall Lakes School looks exactly like our school. If they need to, they can go into the lobby and measure the showcase to see if the object would fit inside. It's almost as if the children are doing their sleuthing at the scene of the crime.

Once the class has decided by vote which valuable object was stolen, each detective pair must fill out an insurance claim form with a description and picture of the valuable item.

Then the detectives do some real sleuthing. They need to learn how the crook could steal a valuable object from the front showcase without being seen by anyone in the school. In order to do this, they have to observe exactly what happens at a school at 10:00 A.M., the time the crime was committed. They do this by donning their disguises and fanning out through the school at 10 A.M. Each partner has a preassigned spot. It might be a classroom, the nurse's office, a bathroom, or the kitchen. The entire school is covered, but the plum assignment is the front lobby with the all-important showcase.

The detectives are instructed to "blend in with the wallpaper" and take careful notes for fifteen minutes. They are told to write down everything they see and hear. We warn all staff that our children will be spying on them and ask that they ignore our detectives if that is possible. It is quite a sight to see the kids "blending in" while wearing funny wigs, hats, and sunglasses. When the fifteen minutes are up, all detectives return to the classroom and share their reports. Little do unsuspecting visitors wandering through our halls at 10:00 A.M. that day know that they are under the intense scrutiny of forty-eight detectives and that their every move is being recorded and discussed at length.

Another favorite activity is the observation test. For this activity we are lucky to have the help of a school secretary who enjoys dressing up even more than I do. On the day of the observation test, she disguises herself so well that her own mother wouldn't recognize her. She tiptoes around our classroom acting strange and devious. She never says a word, and the children don't speak to her. We warn the children beforehand that a stranger will arrive in our room but they must not speak to "him." Instead, they must observe how he looks, and watch every move he makes. We want them to take notes, and we tell them how important it is for detectives to notice details. The notes are incorporated into eyewitness reports. Later, when we read the detectives' reports, we are always struck by how the descriptions of the stranger vary. This is a difficult assignment.

Next, each pair must reconstruct the crime. Once they have figured out how the culprit might have stolen the item and escaped with it, they draw a map of the school and trace the path of the crime with little footprints or arrows. They must label important areas and include a key with the map. The maps are interesting, and we display them for all to see.

Each detective pair invents four suspects who would normally be found in a school. They sketch a picture of each suspect and write the name, motive, and connection with the school under each sketch. When the children want to use names of actual teachers at our school, they are told quite firmly that even though Kendall Lakes looks like their school it is not, and they must create the suspects themselves.

Each team is responsible for writing a report telling how the crime was committed and naming the villain. Then we create a play using the same stolen item. We choose a detective and suspects from the characters created by the children. The play usually takes another month to prepare and present, but it definitely is an optional activity and not necessary for the success of the simulation.

Sometimes plays just naturally evolve from the process of simulations, since the plot and the characters are already in place. In fact when role-playing is a part of your daily routine, at times it will seem as if you and your class are characters in a drama with improvised dialogue. It is a small step from enacting a board meeting in the classroom to enacting a board meeting on the stage in front of an audience. It is, however, a step that children enjoy.

Creating a new persona is very much a part of the world of childhood. Spend any time at all with a group of children engaged in play and see how they interact with each other. Think back to your own childhood. How did you play? Weren't you and your friends immersed in a world of make-believe? I know I was. Children thrive on make-believe. In this chapter I have attempted to show how I use the children's love of fantasy to help them learn. I believe it has enriched the lives of the children in my classes. It certainly has given us many laughs. If you haven't tried it yet, look through your closet, find an old hat and a funny jacket, and give it a whirl.

As for Assessment

Evaluation is an ongoing process. I begin to observe and take mental notes as the children enter my classroom each morning. Although I may not be jotting my observations down, I am constantly watching and thinking and entering information about individuals into the storehouse of information in my mind. I carefully note how they react to each other, their written responses, what they say, and how they act. I question and compare notes with other teachers who work with my children during the course of the day. The evaluation process doesn't stop at the end of the day, but continues when I reflect about the day's events after the children leave, and sometimes keeps me awake during the night.

In my town, we are required to prepare three report cards during the school year. In order to complete these narrative reports, I examine writing folders and accumulated work for each child and compare early work to the most recent. I have a good idea from daily observations of how each child is doing.

I want my children to think about their own academic and social growth, too. It is important that they be aware of their own progress, so every time I write a report card I ask them to do the same. They look over their writing folders and accumulated work and then compose their own narrative reports. When parents come for conferences, I share these original and interesting report cards with them. Often, the children's self-assessments are more revealing than mine.

Pat Reflects—

My hat's off to Judy! Her innovation and creativity in developing so many forms of role-playing across so many areas of the curriculum give all of us inspiration. Her chapter reminds us that the excitement children experience when they play can continue for learners of all ages.

Like Judy, I too enjoy make-believe. Judy's recount of her work with simulations reinforces the power of having the teacher involved in all learning. The teacher needs to be part of the classroom community, too. I got tired of being the paper-passer-outer, the observer to the students' involvement in simulations and inquiry. The role of "facilitator" may work for some, but I felt left out when I played that role, when I stood on the fringes watching it all happen for my students. That feeling was what prompted me to start using simulations for learning in upper elementary school. Once I dived in and gave myself the joy of being part of the fun, I began to see the potential for truly engaged excitement for all of us.

Judy was braver than I am—she dressed up. In spite of my theater background, I never dressed up, and neither did my students. Perhaps it was because they were sixth graders, more likely it was because we just never got around to it. My students, like Judy's, walked around the school building, talking to each other in character, using their current simulation names, spontaneously. I think they would have taken it as far as I was willing to have it go. And, come to think of it, they may have been dressed up—especially when we were modern-day archeologists on our way to Egypt—and I just never knew it. I know at their age, wrapped in the power of a game, I would have gotten dressed in the morning thinking of my character: "What would Dr. So-and-So, archeologist—me—wear on a day like this?" I do know that many of my sixth graders were deeply immersed in their characters, well beyond the confines of the class activities.

As I mentioned in Chapter 1, Vygotsky believed that play provides to learners its own zone of proximal development; that in play children can do things they could not normally do alone and become, as it were, "a head taller." This becomes especially strong when children—and adults—are invited to take on the role of someone whom they see as already invested with power. Thus, when my sixth graders were pretending to be archeologists with advanced degrees, they seemed to believe themselves capable of great research. I found their work to be better than that which they did under their own names, as "regular old classwork." The artificially elevated status that we achieve in a simulation lends us power and credibility, and other opinions of ourselves as doers may fade into the background as we see ourselves in a new persona capable of great things.

This power of imagination serves me every day. Although I no longer invent names for myself in play, I am now given roles to play in my adult life, and often those roles are ones that are new to me. When I must perform in this new role, as this "new" person, I find myself asking, "What would someone do in this case? What does the chair of a committee [for instance] do in this situation? How does a college teacher act, dress, talk?" And in playing these new roles, I draw on my experience, my intuition, and my imagination, exactly as I would do in play and exactly as my students did in simulations. And, like them, being invested with a role to play lends me power, and I am able to do things I did not know I could do. I become, as it were, "a head taller." Pat Cordeiro, plain old person, doing dishes, watching TV, only has the capabilities to do big and important things because I am able to see myself in different roles. That envisioning of myself in different roles and the competence that follows both flow directly from my ability to imagine, pretend, and play.

I believe, with Judy, that the work we do in the world of imagination is some of the most important work we do in schools. Yet it is the most lacking of all elements in upper elementary school. I believe that through work with imagination, we give children the practice and the ability to see themselves in new roles and with new capabilities. With those new visions of themselves come new possibilities and stronger competencies.

Our role as teachers is central as it validates the work going on and cements the bond between us and our students. As Judy puts it, "I don't underestimate the importance of my enjoyment."

Carli came into teaching because of her life as a mother. Her second child was a special education student. Through her experiences, Carli witnessed the effect of good teachers, and appreciated how these very special teachers helped children—her child—to get through each year. They saw his potential, the promise of what he could be, and focused on this rather than on his problems. This vision, this ability to see the potential in each child, became Carli's vision and influenced her to continue her own education and become a teacher of special needs children.

As a child, Carli was taught through drill, practice, and rote memorization. Her teacher-training emphasized the same techniques, leaving little room for teacher or child self-expression. The first few years of her teaching career were spent in a substantially separate setting where she used the techniques handed down to her from her teachers. Carli found it difficult to follow the daily regimen of workbooks and dittos, of twenty minutes for language or spelling. She was drawn to search for other ways to teach.

Carli had a sense of what she wanted and needed to do for her own self-expression as well as for the self-esteem, growth, and development of her students. And so she began to gradually change her style of teaching. She observed other teachers, read professional books, attended conferences and workshops, and tentatively tried new ways of drawing on her own learning style while drawing out each child's individuality. She took what she observed and learned from others and reshaped it until it felt comfortable, until it fit. And when it fit, she wore it for awhile. At the same time, she was constantly driven to stretch her own comfort level. Over the years she's kept the basic teaching style that she developed, but she's always trying new ideas—constantly retailoring her style.

Carli is committed to sharing her process of change with teachers who want to change. The way she continues to grow is by working with others in consulting work, and by presenting teacher workshops on how to develop integrated curriculum and use poetry in all subject areas. These interactions and exchanges of information impact how she continues to change as a teacher and as an individual.

And so Carli came to Henry Barnard and to her third-grade classroom where she's been for the past four years. The following teacher profile is a reflection on how the students and Carli continue to grow and change together.

She says, "We're never finished with our promise."

CHAPTER FIVE

Reflecting on the Rain Forest in the Third Grade

Carli Carrara

It's the last week of school, and I watch the children scattered about the room, in groups or alone, finishing up stories, writing in response journals, discussing a book. Three boys are engrossed in drawing a detailed map of the underground home of the rats of NIMH. Another group of children is illustrating rain forest stories they wrote and published for the kindergartens and first grades. Everyone is busy. I remember when they first came into my room in September, unsure of what the third grade was going to be like. We are in the "intermediate" wing, considered the "transition" grade between the primary and upper grades, so it's difficult for them not only to begin third grade but to physically move around the corner, to find themselves in the wing with the "big kids."

As I listen to the hum of activity, I think about the exploration I've done, studying with Pat Cordeiro. I remember how she opened up her library to me, saying take what you want, what you need, and emphasizing that this time of studying should be what I wanted it to be, what I needed in order to grow. I had accepted her invitation. Over the weeks of study I read many books and articles on literacy and language. I learned so much from reading and from reflecting on what I read as well as on what I do in my classroom. I spent weeks forming and reforming; questioning who I am as a teacher and as a person; reflecting on how my experiences, philosophy, and education affect my teaching. My dialogues with Pat have helped me to better define my concept of the teacher I am and the one I want to become. I see this concept of "good teacher" as an ever-changing one that will continue to evolve as I move through the lives of my students and as they move through mine. Reading about the experiences and theories of others has helped me affirm my beliefs about how to teach. While I read, I recalled the small daily celebrations that make teaching so rewarding,

77

the light in children's eyes when they truly "see." Each article, each book, was a mirror, a reflection of what I saw during my day, what I did well, what I wished I hadn't done or had done better, and what I'd like to see myself doing.

Each class is so different, has its own personality. It takes time to get a handle on it, so we spend the first couple of months getting to know each other and building a sense of trust so they will feel free to take risks as learners, to explore. And explore they do.

My curriculum is based on community, on the interconnectedness and interdependence of all things, and on diversity as the necessary catalyst in learning about ourselves and others. These concepts are the center of all the integrated units I have developed on the field, the family, whales, the ocean, and the rain forest.

I've always use myths, fables, and legends throughout the year to demonstrate the universality of stories and human experiences. They contain the archetypes that children recognize across cultures in stories they read and create. And create they do. All the language they've heard and read surfaces in their writing and speaking. I read the original versions to them, no watered-down text. Then we looked at the structure of myths and decided what we needed to do to make our own myths. The students wrote page after page, invented all sorts of characters— heroes, heroines, monsters—fantastic names for people and places, and conflicts that needed to be resolved.

This is quite a contrast from the times years ago when I would ask my students on the first day of school to write about their summer vacation. They'd sit for what seemed forever, staring at the paper, the ceiling, the floor, finally squeezing out a few simple sentences. I've since learned that asking children to model their writing after something I've read to them or something they've read on their own is the key to opening up a magical box. So I read to them all year, from every genre— myths, legends, fairy tales, poetry, mysteries like *The House of Dies Drear* (Hamilton 1984), and adventures and stories of family like *The Hundred Penny Box* (Mathis 1986) and *The Jungle Book* (Kipling 1987). All of these deal with the many layers of humanity. I use poetry throughout the curriculum, beginning each day with a Poem-of-the-Day and usually focusing on a theme we are studying, such as the sea or the rain forest. I read classic as well as contemporary poetry. We look at the techniques the poets used and we try them out—repetition, rhyme, meter, and alliteration. We write poems of apology after reading W. C. Williams's poem "This is Just to Say"; we write shape poems of whales, snowflakes, rocks, and trees; we write persona poems in which we become a fruit or a vegetable and speak of life underground or how it feels to hang from a tree. All the time, the children's language is growing richer, more complex.

Marnie Schwartz (1990) speaks about allowing children to "step inside the skins of villains and heroes—connect to literature—know themselves" (32). I must believe this, because the children tell me this is true. They speak of being that person they're writing about, of making all the things in the story "be happening to me."

All the students in my room think of themselves as writers. When I ask them what it takes to be a good writer they say "concentration," "imagination"; they consider themselves writers—good writers. Mastering the mechanics doesn't seem to be a major requirement for them because "you can always get help with spelling and punctuation," and as for handwriting, well, "you can always type it." If you don't have good ideas and a good imagination and concentration, you won't be a good writer. At least, that's what they believe.

When I read to them from any genre, they say to themselves, "I can do that!" They understand that the more they write, the better they write. When I asked each of them what made them a better writer this year, the first response was, "I wrote a lot." Then they said they read a lot, which helped them write better, and they all agreed that "the stories and poems you read to us helped—all the different language." They never realized that there were so many ways to use language. By exposing them to many forms and encouraging them to play with language, I've helped them now to feel more comfortable. They learned that language is not something written in stone, that it can be shaped and formed to be or say whatever they want. They began to see it as a tool to use in order to express their thoughts and feelings. We have become a community of readers and writers. Our language is the language of literature in all its forms. We talk about it, write about it, act it out, and draw it.

Immersed in my own professional reading, I found myself saying, "Yes, I've seen that in my class or in a particular student." I began taking notes about children in my class and decided to develop a Reading and Writing Interview. I thought I could predict what each child would say. Some did respond the way I thought they would—most didn't. I hoped my students would talk about the enrichment, stories, poems, discussions, and questions I asked them to ask themselves when they wrote or read. Most of them did say all the stories and poems helped, but when they talked about the questions *I* asked, they were no longer *my* questions. The children talked about the questions "I ask myself." The questions were now internalized; the students owned them. I was delighted. This was growth!

The students said these questions helped them make their stories more interesting, "not just bunches of words stuck together." They had learned that ideas had to fit together. They put more thought into their work. "People like to listen and read my stories now," they said. They had moved through what Vygotsky calls "the zone of proximal development" to that of constructing and owning their own knowledge.

As I administered the interviews and tried to write down what each child said, I realized several things. First, I needed a tape recorder. Each question unleashed such a torrent of responses that the questions I had so carefully selected became irrelevant. The children just spoke about how they learned to read and write, when and where they read and write, and how they became better readers and writers. They didn't distinguish that much between the two. They felt one depended on the other. They saw themselves as readers *and* writers. I couldn't write fast enough. I realized that some of my questions were confining. I found out a lot about each child, things I didn't know—and if I had known them at the beginning of the year, I would have approached each child differently. I decided I would use a tape recorder next time, use more open-ended questions, let the children lead the way, and use the interview at the beginning and end of the year.

In my own studies, I learned about language variations, about how errors in language reflect the developmental stages of the child. Now I was able to look at Mary's case of leaving off the final consonants when she writes as probably being typical of her home language use. I looked at Maria's work with new eyes, noting that her use of negatives perhaps reflected her knowledge of Spanish grammar, which was spoken in her home. I saw Lee's example of leaving out the copula "to be" and the omission of final consonants in words as a potential reflection of his first language, Chinese. I also was able to see the ways each child used language socially, and now understood why Lee never looked me in the eye, always responded with only "yes" and "no," and never volunteered an answer. His reluctance to ask for help or answer a question might originate in culture.

My professional readings brought back my own memories of six years ago when I had struggled, trying to find time to "do" the language textbook chapters—in order—and the worksheets that went with them. I remembered how I resented having to stop in the middle of an interesting activity like watching the bullfrog someone bought in, its emerald eyes bulging out at us as he sat in the terrarium chugging away. We had to stop because it was "time for language." "All right now," I'd say, "we have to stop. We'll watch the frog later." Every time I said this, I'd cringe and the children would groan. I knew this had to be wrong, this stopping of an activity because we *had* to do "a subject." So, little by little, I changed my teaching. As time went on, we drew the frog or the ants or the butterflies on the back of all the old dittos I had accumulated. I was driven to find new ways of teaching, to search out other teachers, and so I used my professional days to visit other schools, other classrooms, to watch process writing in action. I attended workshops and conferences on process writing, always drawn by the inner knowledge of what I felt was right. I knew the learning-disabled children I was teaching weren't learning as well as they could. They struggled through workbooks, bored by the repetition and drill and the dull basal readers.

I remembered how it had been for me in school. I found it difficult, if not impossible, to produce what my teachers valued. I was always being sent to the office for talking, for being out of my seat. All through high school I struggled, dealing with the rote memorization of teacher-dictated facts, no questions allowed, no drawings, no dialogues, no puppets, no dioramas. It wasn't until I was over thirty that I realized I was "okay," that the way I learned best was not wrong, just different from all the left-brained requirements set up by schools to evaluate and teach.

Now I sit here and look at my classroom, at the kapok tree we built as the centerpiece for our rain forest. The creation of this rain forest began with us all watching a video called "Jungle" from the TV series "The Living Planet." In the first scene, David Attenborough is sitting in the uppermost layers of the canopy in a rain forest. He's perched on a sling chair discussing the diversity of plants and animals found there, as well as the conditions necessary for survival. He then moves slowly through each layer, examining each one until he reaches the floor. This video gives children an overview of the various ecosystems found in the rain forest. The photography is excellent and whets children's appetites for more, teasing them to explore to the depth we will do.

My room contains a large personal library of resources, which includes books, both fiction and nonfiction, tapes, videos, posters, and computer software on the rain forest. We examine the materials individually or in small groups, then each child decides which plant or animal to study and writes a report on its habits and habitat. The report is done in the form of an interview, each child dressing up as their creature and then being interviewed by another student who acts as "reporter."

During the five or six weeks of this unit, all activities revolve around the rain forest. Mornings are spent researching and participating in various math, reading, and writing activities related to the subject.

Since we've adopted an acre of real rain forest, we measure out an acre on the soccer field to get an idea of its size. We measure the height of the trees and their girth, examine their leaves and their bark, and measure the temperature in the various leaves of the woods behind our school and the humidity. We learn about what makes the different types of soil, and we test them. We examine rotting logs and leaves to investigate the processes of decay and the variables that make it occur faster. We read stories; write poems; and study the geographical locations of rain forests around the world, the indigenous peoples who live there, and the effect that the lack of habitat has on their lives. We learn about the products of the rain forest, and how we use them for food and medicine, clothing, and furniture.

In the afternoons we build the 3D mural and the kapok tree. These activities are accomplished in small cooperative groups and/or individually. By the time they're ready to begin this unit in April, the students have already completed four intensive units on the family, the field, whales, and the coral reef. They are used to working cooperatively in groups, learning from each other, and teaching their peers.

Some children choose to paint the mural; others create plants, flowers, leaves, and creatures from recycled materials. Still others choose to construct the tree from large sheets of corrugated cardboard. They work methodically, interacting with each other, often changing jobs or helping someone who's having difficulty.

One year they decided to put on a play for the school using their rain forest as a "set." They decided to do their own interpretation of Lynn Cherry's (1990) book, *The Great Kapok Tree*. They added roles to include the creatures they had researched and rewrote lines to include the information they had learned. After two or three years the play became a given. It was part of the school culture. It was what you did in third grade. Being the audience for several years built an expectation of "it's my turn." Now it differs each year reflecting the interests of each class.

In this classroom, information is presented in various formats to accommodate the learning styles of all students. Videos, slides, and brief lectures using pictures and/or diagrams, handouts, and vocabulary lists all introduce new terms that will help the students understand what we are studying. Throughout the unit, the children are encouraged to develop process and problem-solving skills as they build the mural and the tree, fashion the creatures, and work at play. They feel at ease and are certain of success as they have the opportunity to develop creative solutions to the problem presented. Using imagination as well as process skills, a child can carry an activity to the furthest of her or his ability without being penalized for not reaching a particular endpoint.

At the end of six weeks, the classroom is a rain forest. It is a collective representation of their understanding of the relationships within this ecosystem. It is a shared reference, commonly created, that demonstrates and integrates their research physically, visually, and socially. It grows from floor to ceiling. The kapok tree is held up by buttresses and extends into the center of the room. Behind it is a mural that runs the width of the room. Lianas drape down from its branches, which are strung from the ceiling by fishing line. Bromeliads nestle in the crotches of the limbs. Orchid frogs, snakes, and animals of all kinds found in the rain forest are here. My students made all these beautiful things based on what they learned by reading, listening, watching, talking, and cooperating. Now they place themselves around the base of the tree, reading, talking, and drawing under its branches. The light in the room has a greenish glow from the rain forest paintings on the windows. The children researched all the plants and the animals, the children each going in their own direction, at their own rate. They studied the indigenous peoples of the rain forest, cultures from all over the world; and they sold "Rain Forest Crunch" at Open House to raise money for Cultural Survival, a group that helps native peoples of the world. They made posters to hang around the school and performed their own version of the book *The Great Kapok Tree* for parents and other students in the school. No one "failed" the rain forest. They were completely engaged in learning and teaching others about what they had learned. Everyone succeeded.

As wonderful as all this looked to me, something bothered me about it, about "my units." After reading Pat Cordeiro's (1992) book, *Whole Learning*, I know what it is. They're "my units," not the children's, and even though each of the units develops differently each year according to the class, they're still "my units." It's time for me to move on. *We* need to generate the curriculum together because, as I said before, each class has its own personality that needs to be recognized and allowed to develop as fully as possible. So now I'm looking forward to September, when we'll do what Pat calls a "generative curriculum." I'm excited and frightened—excited at the possibilities of becoming a learner with my students and afraid of the unknown and the apparent lack of structure. I've always had units strung together through my year, and we seemed to move logically from one to the other. The connections were obvious to me, but were they obvious to all the children? If I truly believe in developmentally appropriate teaching and that each child needs to construct his or her own concepts, I must allow them to do this by giving them time and space to construct. Secondly, I must model learning. As Pat says:

> If I and my students are to make sense out of what we're trying to understand, then I must be the first and foremost learner. Only when I see myself in that way can any demonstration of modeling I do be authentic. Demonstrating how to learn something without actually learning anything quickly becomes an empty exercise. For I too am a learner with a history. (Cordeiro 1994, 5)

I too will benefit from looking at myself as a lifelong learner giving to myself those gifts I give to my students.

I see my journey taking a new course. I want to thank Pat for helping me to see where I was in my journey, where I am as a learner, and for encouraging me to continue to generate my own growth. She's helped me reaffirm my belief that I must "trust my own ways of knowing, value my intuitive knowledge" (Cordeiro 1992). It got me this far.

As for Assessment

Evidence of my students' knowledge is demonstrated by the content of their reports, as well as their poems and stories, which are displayed around the room and the school. I also collect assessment data by observing the processes each child uses to uncover what he or she needs and by noting the dialogues that occur between the children and myself as well as between the children. The collaborative writing of the play and the detailed construction of the rain forest both demand a certain level of understanding and knowledge—a need to know the creatures well enough to answer such questions as: If I'm a fruit bat, do I live in a cave, a tree hollow, or on a plant? Should the marmoset be so close to the leopard? What shape are the leaves of the philodendron, the orchid? How do they grow? How big is a buttress, and why is it on the tree? The children become the creatures and the plants. They understand what is their prey and who is their predator. I record observations in the form of anecdotal notes and place them in the child's portfolio along with photographs taken during the project. At the completion of the unit, each child fills out a self-evaluation sheet that is usually quite candid.

There are no letter grades. We use a checklist accompanied by a narrative to report each child's progress.

Finally, the children's understanding of this ecosystem becomes obvious when we compare it to our previous unit on the coral reef. The children note their similarities and their differences: the fact that they're both multileveled, have a multitude of species, and have varying temperatures and amounts of light—all of which affect and determine the types of creatures that live there.

Throughout this unit the children take an active part in decision making—in the processes of how the unit will progress. They participate actively in what they're learning, accepting the roles and responsibilities as members of a learning community.

References

Attenborough, David. *The Open Ocean: Living Planet, Portrait of the Earth*. Videocassette.

Atwell, Nancie, ed. 1990. *Workshop 2: Beyond the Basal*. Portsmouth, NH: Heinemann.

Cherry, Lynn. 1990. *The Great Kapok Tree: A Tale of the Amazon Rain Forest*. New York: Harcourt Brace.

Cordeiro, Pat. 1992. *Whole Learning: Whole Language and Content in the Upper Elementary Grades*. Katonah, NY: Richard C. Owen.

———. 1994. "Becoming a Learner Who Teaches." In *Teachers Networking* 12 (1).

Hamilton, Virginia. 1984. *The House of Dies Drear*. New York: Macmillan.

Kipling, Rudyard. 1987. *The Jungle Book*. New York: Puffin.

Mathis, Sharon. 1986. *The Hundred-Penny Box*. New York: Puffin.

Newkirk, Thomas, and Nancie Atwell, eds. 1987. *Understanding Writing: Ways of Observing, Learning and Teaching*. Portsmouth, NH: Heinemann.

Schwartz, Marnie. 1990. "The Room in Which Van Gogh Lived." In Nancie Atwell, ed., *Workshop 2: Beyond the Basal*. Portsmouth, NH: Heinemann.

Williams, William Carlos. 1985. *Selected Poems*. New York: New Directions Publishing Corp.

Pat Reflects—

I am always impressed when I talk with Carli or spend time in her room. I think what makes all the difference is her stated philosophy of having a centrality to all she sees happening in the classroom, based on "community, on the interconnectedness and interdependence of all things, on diversity as the necessary catalyst." Many of us have broad themes and concepts that serve to link activities, processes, and content across the school days. We may even have much larger goals that are unstated or that we are unaware of having because we take them for granted. Carli's goal is stated and clearly articulated before she begins the first day. Within this central goal and driving philosophy, the themes are developed.

Carli shows clearly the power of professional reading and talk. In some cases her readings supported work she was already doing, like the work with myths, but in some cases, she discovered new directions, as she did when she initiated the teacher-student interview. And always her readings brought back memories, made connections, and gave her pause to think. Carli's account reminds us of the valuable professional books available for teachers and how powerful they are for our own growth and change. She reminds us of the value of having someone to talk to about the reading and thinking.

Carli has experienced the power in administering teacher-student interviews and, now armed with tape recorder and pencil, she will use it as a beginning- and end-of-the-year tool. I have found that many teachers have a similar, positive response to this tool. I now ask teachers in coursework to interview children on the subject we're studying, usually language arts and reading. We have had less success with the teacher-student interview process in social studies, primarily because some elementary school children have so little to report. Still, that's a lesson for teachers, too.

When I ask teachers in coursework to interview their own students about attitudes and experiences in various subjects, they inevitably come away with the same response Carli had. They see the value of this as an evaluation and planning instrument, and make plans to use it as part of their own program. Teachers and preservice teachers are also sometimes surprised at the responses children give. They often form a new impression of the children's program, for sometimes the responses they collect are uniformly negative. Sometimes the interviews are difficult because students don't have the language for response if they never before have been asked their opinion about the subjects they are studying.

Teachers interviewing at the end of the year as a requirement for my coursework sometimes report feelings of regret that they didn't do this sooner. One commented that as she completed the interviews, she suddenly realized that this was the first time all year that she had sat down with individual students and listened for ten minutes, the time it took for the interview. She said, "Imagine, all year long, I never listened to them for ten minutes."

Carli's students are clearly in control of reading and writing and do have the language of response and reflection. Carli often asks them to talk about their process. She pulls back the curtain of teaching by talking about learning with those most involved—the students. And Carli's classroom resonates with imagination, a recurring theme for me. In her setting, the children are literally immersed in the world they're studying, life inside the rain forest. Imagination and reality travel hand-in-hand in this environment. As Carli notes, it is a "collective representation . . . a shared reference, commonly created." Beyond that, children in Carli's classroom are actively engaged in living their learning process. As they connect reading and writing on a daily basis, Carli says, they become the person they're reading and writing about: They think of the events as if they might "be happening to me." Now Carli will go deeper into her classroom relationships, exploring the richer meaning of a generative curriculum, as she and her children collectively decide how learning will happen in the future. I'm excited at the possibilities, and I hope she'll write about it as she explores her "journey taking a new course."

About Lisa Burley Maras and Bill Brummett

This chapter describes Lisa and Bill's first experience working together. Lisa had been a primary special education teacher. Bill had taught for twenty-seven years in all kinds of classrooms, from elementary to high school. Now they would each have their own third- and fourth-grade, multi-age class. They planned to team together as much as possible.

Both Lisa and Bill were constantly involved in their own independent reading and research. They had discovered that they not only had similar beliefs about learning and teaching, but they also were both interested in exploring similar questions. These included: How do we create a curriculum based on inquiry? How do we create classrooms in which the questions are discovered, and the areas to be explored happen in collaboration with students? Lisa and Bill were no longer satisfied with offering choices within chosen topics. They wanted to create an environment in which the classroom community, teachers and students together, would have choice of topic and choice of direction.

Lisa and Bill consulted the work of Carolyn Burke, Jerome Harste, and Kathy Short most frequently. They especially relied on the book Creating Curriculum *(Short and Burke 1991). They were convinced that this was the way they wanted to, and should, go.*

So, Lisa and Bill were hopeful that they could work together and with their students to create a curriculum based on the real questions that mattered to all of them. Even though they were not sure how this change would happen, they were eager to begin the year. They were hopeful that it could happen, and they knew that they had a fantastic group of young eight- and nine-year-old collaborators. You shall hear their voices throughout this chapter.

CHAPTER SIX

Time for a Change: Presidential Elections in a Grade 3–4 Multi-age Classroom

Lisa Burley Maras and Bill Brummett

A Year of Change

"It's not you and it's not us . . . it's like when you're writing a story and the characters take over. In this class our learning is in charge; our learning takes over."

This student's words describe the change that occurred in our classrooms over the course of one school year. This is our story of how a particular inquiry interest led all of us, students and teachers, into creating our own curriculum. We had made the decision to study something that really mattered to us. All that we did was based on our questions and interests.

Where We Started

We, the teachers, had decided to begin the year with a study of life cycles. We felt it was a perfect topic, and fall was a perfect time. Children are naturally interested in plants and animals, especially baby animals. There were plenty of insects and spiders around that they could get their hands on. It would also fit in with our overnight camping trip at a nearby state park. Loads of questions were bound to occur that would set us off either individually, in small groups, or as an entire class observing and studying plants and animals around us. We felt we had come up with the ideal theme with which to start the year.

As teachers we felt we were providing our students with a very open theme through which we could offer many choices. These choices would allow the children to come up with some of their own ideas. There was research to do, books and articles to read, experiments to perform, observations to make, hypotheses to formulate, and notes to take. Children could present their findings in many different ways. Research results could be organized into written or oral reports. Demonstrations could be planned. Charts and other visuals could be created. We felt that the possibilities were endless and would keep us, and the children, motivated and involved.

Time for a Change

And so we began the year. We worked hard to immerse ourselves in our life cycles theme. But it was September 1992, a presidential election year. We found that the constant bombardment of commercials, debates, and all the coverage from TV, radio, and newspapers prevented us from focusing our full attention on our life cycles theme. We found ourselves spending more and more of our classroom time discussing the election, campaign issues, and candidates. Because the talk was so rich, our conversations kept us riveted for very lengthy discussions. As teachers we valued our kids being so involved and interested in the topic, but as teachers we also knew we had to take the initiative.

When we sensed what was happening, we knew that we needed to share our thoughts with the students. We were spending more and more of our class time discussing the election. Some of our morning meetings had grown to over an hour in length. Although we were pleased with how things were going, we knew that we could not continue in this way. We were not finding enough time to really get into our study of life cycles.

That is the view we posed to our students. After sharing our perspective, we placed it in their hands. They quickly got involved in defining the situation as they saw it. Realizing that it could not continue the way it was, they began posing problems and solutions, as the following conversation demonstrates.

Russell: We could keep trying to do both. We can work on life cycles and the election.
Meryl: No. That's too much to do. That's the problem we're having now.
Matt: Why don't we just work on the election then?
Several children: Yeah!
Tony: But what about the people who want to keep doing life cycles?
Matt: They could keep doing that if they want to . . .

And so the conversation continued until the children came up with three options and organized a vote. The decision was one vote short of unanimous. We would discontinue our study of life cycles in order to pursue an in-depth study of the 1992 presidential election.

Changing Our Ways

There was immediate enthusiasm and engagement as we all focused on the newspaper and the nightly TV news. Students had already identified with candidates, so debates and arguments sprang up naturally. Some were informed, and others were simply emotional. It soon became obvious that none of us knew as much as we needed to in order to make informed decisions. We decided to take a step back and clarify what we knew about the candidates and the issues.

The butcher paper on the wall took a long time to fill. We found that a lot of what we had written was repetitive and without substance. "Perot has big ears." "Bush lied. He said No More Taxes . . ." and several other similar statements. This brainstorming experience was an eye-opener for the children. They discovered that even though they could spout off some slogans and rhetoric about the election, they really did not know enough to talk—really talk—about it, debate it, or question it. We began to identify some issues to investigate. We found that our concerns focused on five issues: taxes, the economy, health care, the environment, and education. As teachers we could think of several different ways to proceed with this investigation, but again we decided to go to the students before any decisions were made. We would be members of the group discussion, but not the leaders.

After lengthy planning meetings, the class decided that the best way to get into this study would be to divide into three campaign committees for George Bush, Bill Clinton, and Ross Perot. Children selected the candidate they wanted to work for. The initial groups were very lopsided, so children opted to volunteer for another candidate so that each campaign committee had an equal amount of researchers. Each committee was charged with finding out as much as they could about their candidate's position on the issues we decided were most important to us as a class community.

Research occurred in many different ways. At home, parents helped by discussing candidates and issues at the dinner table. They read and discussed the newspaper with their children, and watched and discussed the news and debates. Some parents helped or encouraged children to write down notes and organize what they knew into charts.

In school, we read and discussed newspaper and magazine articles about the election. We began making grids on the wall to organize our information so that quick comparisons could be made. We watched, discussed, and analyzed videotaped debates. We consulted many different information sources such as *Time*; *Newsweek*; *The Congressional Quarterly*; Republican, Democratic, and Independent platform and information sheets; *United We Stand* by Ross Perot; and *Earth in the Balance* by Al Gore. Some parents were also able to help out at school. Some joined our campaign committees, providing assistance with reading and making sense of some of the more complex resources. The parents' participation allowed children the opportunity to gain access to more information and provided yet another group member who would question and collaborate.

As individuals and groups discovered new things about the candidates, we shared with the class as a whole. This was done on a daily basis, and often more than once a day. We found that each conversation led us to more questions. We began to ask questions about our political system. "What is Congress anyway?" "What is the President's job?" "How does the election work?" "What are polls?" "What are debates?"

These questions took us in different directions. We found ourselves needing to create new groups around these new questions and interests. We started to look for new sources, and we began consulting books and other reference materials. One group decided that the best way to find out how an election works is to have one. The group decided to hold a schoolwide mock election. They designed their own system so that they could get everyone involved in the election process. They tallied the votes and shared the results with the entire school.

Another group took it upon themselves to design some polls. They decided on questions to ask and proceeded to poll in the hallways and the cafeteria. They learned about random selection and representative samples. They shared the results with the entire group and discussed at length the items that surprised them. They also determined what the "public" knew about the candidates and what they needed more information on.

Another group was anxious to try their hand at debating. They were surprised to learn that debates had rules and weren't free-for-all shouting matches in which you could hurl insults at your opponent. They soon discovered that they really had to know what they were talking about in order to back up their proposals and convince the voting public. One subgroup formulated questions about the issues, and the other three subgroups prepared to represent their candidates. They set up the date, time, and place and invited classmates and parents to attend.

We found ourselves continually creating new and different groups as we found them necessary. The more we explored, researched, talked, and questioned, the more we needed new groups.

It was while we were immersed in this election study that we discovered we were caught in a cycle, an authoring cycle (Harste, Short, and Burke 1988). We realized that what was happening with us, teachers and students, reflected our questions, concerns, and interests. Our experiences, questions, and interests became our starting point. Together we were originating and becoming the authors and creators of our curriculum. As teachers we realized that this was the authoring cycle in action.

The Authoring Cycle

The authoring cycle was not a new concept for us. We had experienced it as a framework for the language arts, and we knew its generative power. We found it powerful to think of authoring as Harste, Short, and Burke (1988) do, as processes in which we "originate, negotiate, and revise ideas" (5). We had not, however, experienced it as a framework for curriculum. Through our dialogue with students we were led to the power of the cycle. We did not pattern the election study around the authoring cycle, it just occurred naturally (see Figure 6–1).

Our election study authoring cycle began with our *life experiences*. The presidential election was a topic with obvious connections to our lives outside of school. It had real purpose for all of us. As a topic that was valued by society at large, its news surrounded us daily. Real issues, ones we all wanted to study, were the basis of the election study. The topic had a lot of appeal and enthusiasm. Interaction and conversation was a given. What we were discussing in school was validated as we watched TV at night. Conversations that took place at the family dinner table came into the classroom.

We explored our questions in a variety of ways in order to become better informed. Our investigations included reading a variety of sources. We listened to newscasts and followed the debates. Our daily conversations in the classroom gave us the opportunity to share our thoughts and opinions and also to listen to the ideas of others. This *wide exploration* was through collaboration with peers, teachers, parents, and other adults we sought out for specific information.

We collaborated with one another. We shared ideas and formed questions and plans. We talked things out, we listened, we argued, we tried to convince and persuade. During our *collaboration* with others, we often found ourselves forced to reexamine our beliefs and thinking.

FIG. 6–1   Our adaptation of the Authoring Cycle (Short and Burke 1991)

As we learned about and tried to understand the ideas and opinions of others, we often incorporated them into our own thinking.

Classroom meetings—some planned, many spontaneous—served to move our thinking forward. As we presented our new information, views, and opinions, comments from our class forced *reflection and revision*. As we shared what we were learning and thinking, we discovered new questions to pursue and were often led in different directions. We had to formulate new plans. We found ourselves revising our beliefs and discovered that we also changed in this process.

Although the basic study groups were formed around the candidates, splinter groups formed with new purposes as we gathered new information, asked new questions, and set new directions. We shared what we learned in a variety of ways. Each group found their own unique way to *present and share their meaning with others*. We shared as groups and as individuals. Much of our sharing was informal conversation in both small groups and the whole class. Some presentations were more formal, such as the debates in the auditorium and written editorials published in our classroom newspaper.

Students were all trying to find the best way to pursue their questions and carry out their projects. Throughout the process, we continuously reflected on and discussed our work. We all helped each other by sharing what worked, what didn't work, and the roadblocks we faced. We *examined the strategies* we used to research and share our information.

Our election study provided the basis for *invitations to further engagements*. Because of discussions surrounding the presidential elections, a change occurred in our classrooms. It was a change that placed more value on a curriculum that was generated by the entire group and that had relevance in school as well as out of school. Our reflection took us back into our own thinking and moved us on to further engagements and investigations. Even though our focus on the presidential election came to an end, the cycle itself continued. The classroom community had many issues and questions that were brought out in our election study. These questions propelled us into our next study, and this continued through the year. As the year progressed, we focused on such topics as discrimination, prejudice, human rights, the rain forest, regions of the world, and our local community of Genesco, New York. The roots of all these studies can be traced back to our focus on the presidential elections.

Throughout the entire process we found ourselves constantly moving back and forth in exploring, collaborating, reflecting, revising, discovering new questions, and being taken back into our own thinking. We discovered that the authoring cycle functioned as a huge spider web, with strands going from one section to any other section. The web was spun naturally by us, students and teachers, and our questions and needs. Where we functioned in the cycle was determined solely by individual needs or the needs of the group.

It was the questions of the students, along with our willingness to try and allow to happen what we believed was possible, that immersed us in the inquiry cycle. This change came from us and the children. As teachers, our beliefs and understandings about learning made this change possible and desired. The children made it possible as they eagerly embraced the opportunity to pose and pursue their own questions. We all breathed life into the cycle with our passions, questions, and wonderings about the candidates and the election process. As teachers, we also helped keep it going by helping children to see possibilities and directions, and to identify new questions. We, as teachers, found ourselves and our students living what we read and valued.

Learning Takes Over

Many changes occurred in our classrooms once the inquiry cycle took over. We found the whole process to be highly generative. The issues we were studying were powerful and the concerns and questions were ours, so consequently the role we played in our investigations was empowering. We found that creating a curriculum was about empowerment and the roles of teachers and students. It is about who controls what in the classroom and who holds the power. It is about who makes the choices and how decisions are made. In the authoring cycle framework, roles and relationships changed. We watched our students take control of their learning. They learned that their choices and decisions not only mattered, but were necessary. They no longer looked to us to tell them what to do, and they were very aware of their new role as partners with the teacher in the process of creating a curriculum.

Meryl put it this way: "Our learning has taken over. It's not really anyone who's in charge. We're not in charge and Mrs. Maras is not in charge. Because if Mrs. Maras was in charge things would be different."

Once the students acquired voice we could sense their empowerment. They began to look at school and schooling through different eyes.

"Everyone in the class is in charge," stated Rachel.

"That includes us and the teacher," clarified Justin.

"You need everybody, it can't be just one," added Rachel.

The changes of roles for teachers and students were immediately obvious once we were immersed in creating our own curriculum. We all looked at each of us as equal collaborators, and no one was in charge. We valued what we could learn from one another.

"Everybody can help us, not just one person, there's twenty-five of us," Emily observed.

"In a discussion you can get twenty-five ideas, instead of just one. Everyone teaches everyone. Everyone is a teacher," Matt added.

We came to value one another and believe that everyone had something to contribute. We discovered that we could truly learn from one another and that good feedback was not provided solely by the teacher. We learned to appreciate the teacher as a fellow learner, not as the one in complete and sole charge.

Maggie pointed this out and also the fact that she and her peers relished the opportunity to pose their own questions. "Kids' minds. Us.

We decided what to do. You might help us, but you didn't tell us what to do."

Having the opportunity to make real decisions and choices was crucial for this change to occur. We thought we had allowed for real choices before, but in actuality we had only allowed students to select from several options that we offered. In this new process, children began making choices at the most basic level. Now they were creating a curriculum based on their questions and needs. Once the inquiry topic had been decided, it was the inquiry itself that guided all their other decisions. They took charge of the whole inquiry process, from posing the initial questions to doing a complete exploration and investigation to sharing their learning with others.

Rachel described how she had taken control of her learning process:

> When you have a choice, it's like you never want to stop. Learning is fun when you want to do it, and you get to do it your way. When you do your own planning and you decide which days you're gonna read, this day you're gonna watch a movie, this day you're gonna do this. Well, I like doing it in any way, in any order that I can, because I do it when I need to and not when the teacher says.

The students became involved in framing the questions and issues, and the topic had obvious meaning to everyone involved. As teachers we became participants and not the ones who determined the objectives and then designed lessons to accomplish those objectives. We entered the dialogue and became members of the community generating questions and knowledge. We contributed to the understanding of a topic without taking over ownership of that topic. The role of teacher and student became more fuzzy.

Importance of Conversations

As teachers, we had always valued conversation as an important and necessary part of learning. Yet it took this experience to help us realize how critical it is for maintaining and continuing the authoring cycle.

Adam described the importance of talking this way: "If you really talk and if it's something the kids want to do, and if you REALLY talk for a long time you get into the juicy stuff. Then you start getting serious."

We heard Adam's point. Time to talk, really talk, was not only necessary, but critical, for all our learning. We, teachers and students, had always valued opportunities to share and present our work with each other. But our sharing was changing. We were going far beyond telling. We were sharing because it helped us to rethink, wonder, question, and see things from a different angle, with new eyes. Most importantly, we found our conversations leading us to ever more questions. We discovered that when we had ample time to talk, we were able to get to our real questions, to the things that really mattered to us. When our students were provided time to talk about their own questions, they were driven to act on them. They were eager to understand what was going on around them. They worked on building their understanding through interaction with those around them.

In the following conversation, several children commented on how necessary they felt it was to have time to talk to others.

Meryl: You need to talk to people. You can't tell a book what you think. There's no one to share your ideas with. But when you're at a meeting you feel like a real person, you're out there.

Ashlee: Even if people disagree with you.

Kevin: It's okay, because you get other people's opinions.

Tom: There's no right or wrong.

Stephen: When it's coming from a person you are more interested in it and it's like put in your mind. You think about it more.

These comments demonstrate how comfortable all of us were with one another and how we respected one another, and how we were confident that others would listen to us and take us seriously. This trust allowed all of us to take risks and share ideas freely without ridicule. We felt supported and valued. We looked forward to sharing our ideas so that we could receive the input of others.

Tony: When we have meetings, you get to hear comments about what you did.

Matt: We can hear comments that help us.

Todd: Saying "Good job!" doesn't help.

Matt: Questions make us think. We need comments that help us.

The students began to view our discussions as opportunities to hear not only comments, but questions too. They took the comments and questions from others seriously and used them to push their own thinking. They were serious about their work and expected others to be serious in their feedback. They came to value the questions that would push their thinking and their work and make it better. Positive comments like "I liked the way you did . . ." and "That's really good . . ." were just not enough anymore. They wanted to be pushed, and they expected everyone to help.

Making Connections

We discovered that our conversations were the glue that held it all together and helped us create new understandings.

Lexie: We learn every time we have a discussion. We can go from Antarctica to the food pyramid.
Justin: When you are in a discussion you don't only talk about that topic.
Tony: It's like we start talking about all kinds of things.
Rachel: Yeah. And you learn how it's all connected.

This is what the authoring cycle has done for us. It has helped us see, and make, the connections to our learning and to our lives. Our learning was serious. We made our choices and decisions seriously, based on what really mattered to us. We weren't learning for school. We were learning for ourselves because that was what we wanted and needed.

Reflections

Although many things, talking, meetings, research, reading, writing, and other activities we were engaged in throughout this election study were similar to activities that occurred in our classrooms in the past, there was one major difference. In our study of the presidential elections, our children, and we as teachers, were empowered. We were in charge. As teachers we were not teaching specific books or topics, or a collection of facts predetermined and dictated from a source outside the classroom. We were delving into questions that really mattered to us, when they mattered. All our voices were heard, and true choices were made. Never before had we extended choice to this level; never before had our talking led to such questions; never before had our learning become so self-propelled, taking us on and on.

In all of this, the function of curriculum changed. Curriculum was not something we were covering—it was something we were creating. We have learned that any curriculum reflects what is valued, and in this authoring cycle framework, it is our questions, our wonderings, and our processes that are valued.

We look back at this election study as an invitation to ourselves and each other—an invitation to establish new relationships, new power structures, and new courses of study. It was an invitation to question previous ways of doing things, to see the curriculum in a different light, to use the authoring cycle as a framework.

It took this election experience with the children in order for us to truly understand the authoring cycle. It took the two of us as teachers beyond our books and talk and put us into action. We were learners, and we realized that we had all that we needed to change. In *Creating Curriculum* (Short and Burke 1991) Jerome Harste said that "one must see the teacher as a learner and recognize that all the resources we need to change are already at hand. The process begins with curiosity, involves risk, and ends in connected knowing" (xi). That is not only what we watched happen with our children, but it was also what happened to us as teachers.

As for Assessment

The authoring cycle, with its power and energy, became our framework for evaluation. We no longer viewed assessment and evaluation as something that comes at the end of a learning experience. For us they occurred at all stages of the study—from our first wonderings and formulation of questions, through our active engagement, to our final products, and beyond to new topics. Assessment constantly functioned to support learners by enabling them to move beyond their current understandings. We viewed assessment and evaluation from multiple perspectives: students, teachers, collaborative groups, administrators, and parents.

We would argue that evaluation is the mechanism that can and should help learners move beyond the present. It provides an opportunity to interrogate existing values (Harste in Crafton and Burke 1994) and puts learners in a position to experience the world with a new sense of what we believe and a heightened understanding of who we are (Crafton and Burke 1994).

Did we ever interrogate our existing values and move to a heightened understanding of who we are! The authoring cycle proved to be a transformative experience that changed the way we—students, teachers, as well as some parents and administrators—all look at school and our role in school. Classroom dynamics and curricular decisions would never be the same. Self-esteem was bolstered as we all became part of a community whose decisions were driven by our conversations— conversations that reinforced a sense of community, established each member as a creator of knowledge, and strengthened our individual and collective voices. We changed from passive recipients of a curriculum to authors of one where engagement and continuity with our lives, and the act of doing by empowered students and empowered teachers, was valued and encouraged. We were not the same people. We had changed, and our concept of school had changed. For an entire year we were naturally and effortlessly propelled to new studies. Even one year later, former students are still involved in dialogue and studies they had begun in our classrooms. That is convincing assessment.

In our final analysis we cannot limit assessment only to what content, skills, and processes the children were involved in. We have to take it much further to evaluating our view of the curriculum, our classroom environment, and the roles of teachers and students.

The authoring cycle began to drive our classrooms, our curriculum, and our own professional investigations and development. Throughout the entire year, we, as teachers, were involved in our own authoring cycle. The importance of collaboration and conversation, and the powers of voice, choice, and reflection, help us examine assumptions that guide our practices as we continue to change our views of learners, learning, teaching, and curricula. Short and Burke (1991) have helped us learn that change in the classroom comes from within, not from without, and that we must take responsibility for change. And, perhaps most importantly, only when learners support each other from the inside can powerful curricular changes be made.

References

Crafton, L., and C. Burke. 1994. "Inquiry-Based Evaluation: Teachers and Students Reflecting Together." *Primary Voices* K–6. 2 (2):2–7.

Harste, J., K. Short, and C. Burke. 1988. *Creating Classrooms for Authors*. Portsmouth, NH: Heinemann.

Short, K., and C. Burke. 1991. *Creating Curriculum: Teachers and Students as a Community of Learners*. Portsmouth, NH: Heinemann.

Pat Reflects—

Lisa and Bill accomplish so much in their team-taught classrooms it astonishes me. They not only listen to the learning going on around them and validate the young learners they work with, but they also listen so closely to each other, speaking with one voice and thinking with two like minds. And in the process, they channel learned theory to enhance and augment the process, such as seeing Short and Burke's authoring cycle at work in the classroom.

As I read Lisa and Bill's account of their shift in curriculum focus and all that flowed from that shift, I am impressed all over again with the power of combining inquiry and a generative curriculum. Because of their flexibility in planning and curriculum, Lisa and Bill were able to accommodate the vitality in their classroom, generated by the elections, even though they had previously been convinced that the life cycles theme was the most appropriate, "a very open theme through which we could offer many choices." It's hard to give up those plans, especially when they have been meticulously developed by two teamed teachers who care very much about education and their students.

But it is in the nature of inquiry to be generative. And for teachers who respect the power of inquiry, as Lisa and Bill do, it is not possible to ignore the direction of interest in the classroom. Nor is it possible to pursue a path of learning without involving students. To do any less would be to objectify students in the classroom, placing their will outside the realm of consideration, making them powerless. But as Lisa and Bill point out, sharing planning and curricular decision making with students is not only at the heart of good teaching and effective learning, but also determines the nature of relationships in the classroom. As control is shared, classrooms become truly democratic.

I find it particularly interesting in practical terms that groupings changed as their work went on. Some who are schooled in notions of stable cooperative grouping may find it particularly noteworthy that these two teachers-in-service found themselves continually needing new groupings. The impetus for change was not that the teachers needed to control social relationships in the classroom, a practice some of us have indulged in, but rather that the ongoing inquiry required different sets of explorers. Children affiliated with one prong of inquiry at one point might find themselves later venturing in different directions from each other. As the inquiry wound its way forward into new territory, so the groupings would change.

Lisa and Bill point to the power of teachers entering into a learning partnership with students. As a class, they all became "authors and creators of [the] curriculum." Lisa and Bill make powerful and important points when they discuss the subsequent curriculum and learning that flowed from their study of the electoral process. In fact, students did not stop learning about the topic simply because it ended in the classroom. Rather, students continued on their own. Believing that units of inquiry end because school says so is a fantasy of a written curriculum and has nothing to do with the life of children's minds. In fact, Lisa and Bill found that studies continued long after the classwork had ended and that subsequent units of study were related naturally and concretely by children, both in and out of the classroom.

Lisa and Bill also uncover a problematic feature of shared curriculum when they report: "We thought we had allowed for real choices before, but in actuality we had only allowed students to select from several options that we offered." Garth Boomer (1992) also discussed the problems inherent in curricula in which "teachers who still retain the significant, ultimate powers often pretend to divest themselves of power by giving limited decision-making opportunities to the children" (6). In these situations, students may choose from options, but are not free to reject *all* options. Further, Garth argues, such "learning packages demand little creative, individual, teacher and learner contributions" (6).

But Lisa and Bill seem to have accounted for this potential difficulty by recognizing the trap and by involving students and actively seeking a change in the relationships within the classroom. This change was marked by changes in the uses of talk and time in the classroom. Further, they send a message to teachers at all levels about the relevance and nature of assessment as it connects to classroom daily life. They call for assessment that not only considers content, skills, and strategies, but that also looks at curriculum and classroom dynamics. In this view, assessment must continually assess itself. Evaluation not only considers students but also the programs that contain—or constrain—students and teachers within it. Roles and environment are scrutinized as part-and-parcel of classroom life. Through listening to the learning going on around and within them, Lisa and Bill discover a curriculum principle for all of us: "We have learned that any curriculum reflects what is valued."

References

Boomer, Garth. 1992. "Negotiating the Curriculum." In Garth Boomer, Nancy Lester, Cynthia Onore, and Jon Cook, eds. *Negotiating the Curriculum: Educating for the 21st Century*. London: Falmer Press.

Linda's teaching has been greatly influenced by her belief and training in an approach to music education known as Orff Schulwerk, developed by composer Carl Orff. Her school principal also was influential in her growth process by supporting the professional development of the staff and, in her case, by encouraging her to attend all local and regional Orff workshops. Linda says, "These experiences provided me with affirmation of the changes I was making in the classroom and in the music curriculum." Through her participation in these workshops, Linda was invited to chair a committee for a national Orff conference. There she met Frau Orff, widow of Carl Orff. Linda found her delightful and was impressed with Frau Orff's devotion to the Schulwerk: "Frau Orff reflected the heart of the Schulwerk in her elemental, creative approach to what seems to be her life's work—carrying on the work of her husband."

At that national conference, Linda met other teachers who were trying to do what she felt was missing in her teaching. She says, "I felt like I was home, with kindred spirits. There was a special feeling at that conference unlike any other conference I've ever attended." At that same conference she also met Pat Brown, who had worked with Carl Orff and who, years later, worked in collaboration with Linda in a production of Carl Orff's "Carmina Burana." In the late 1980s Linda brought her ideas to "Chapter Sharings," collegial gatherings of Orff Schulwerk teachers from New England. More recently, she is active in local and regional music festivals as a chorus and orchestra manager, and is responsible for music education grades PreK–12 in her town. After twenty-five years of teaching, Linda still looks forward to going to work and, in spite of many obstacles, can't imagine doing anything else. She says, "Working with children from PreK until they're out of high school means that I really get to know them in a unique and special way."

As an Orff educator, Linda doesn't view herself as a "teacher of a method" but, following the beliefs of Carl Orff, speaks in terms of collaborating on an approach that brings children and music together. In the following chapter, she applies that collaborative approach to the integration of two content curricula, music and social studies.

CHAPTER SEVEN

Music and Social Studies in a Medieval Theme in Two Fifth Grades

Linda Squire

"Oh, I thought this was a music class!" The visitor's voice caught our attention, and we all looked up. I followed her puzzled look as she gazed around at the clusters of activity in the multipurpose room. Six boys and girls were seated in a circle, reading the step directions to a dance. Six other students were working at a cafeteria table covered with newspaper; they were putting a new coat of paint on the wooden swords that would be used in the dance. Another table was being used by students who were drawing and coloring characters from the days of Shakespeare. The soft sounds of an alto recorder and lute came from the cassette player. A fourth group was gathering the instruments that would be played to accompany the dancers. This was the fifth-grade general music class, a forty-five minute period of weekly exploration, improvisation, and music making. This day's time was being devoted to the schoolwide social studies theme, the Renaissance. All of these activities were quite normal for this class, in this school, with these curricula in place.

But it wasn't always this way, and this momentary interruption made me reflect on the journey that led to this day. I've been a music teacher for over twenty-five years, seventeen of those years spent in this small, rural community. Most of my early years of teaching involved classroom activities that were born in music methods classes in college. The teacher was the obvious authority in the room and designed, controlled, and directed the students.

I began moving away from this traditional, authoritative pedagogy when I was introduced to the work of Carl Orff, the German composer noted for his gift to the musical education of children, the Schulwerk (schoolwork). Orff stated that "Pedagogy is like a river. As it flows, principles continue to be rediscovered. One can't interfere with the flow of these ideas or contain them in any way" (in Frazee 1985, 19).

Orff Schulwerk places the emphasis on active participation through a variety of media, speech, song, movement, and instruments. Such work begins with speech and the singing voice, drawing on the child's heritage as it is found in nursery rhymes, folks songs, and dances. To this is added body instruments, such as stamping, patting, clapping, and snapping. Movement and drama are then added, followed by the playing of instruments. The instrumentarium is pitched and nonpitched and includes various-sized wood and metal xylophones, recorders, hand drums, and several other percussion instruments. The elements are learned and developed from early childhood and are experienced by participating in activities such as listening, analyzing, performing, reading, and creating. In his "Meditation on Method" (1985), Dr. Arnold Walter of the University of Toronto gives voice to that sense I had of the approach, "Schulwerk is not easy to teach; it cannot be taught mechanically. It involves more than the conscious intellect; it activates a child's spontaneous capacities. It is not a method among other methods; it is not a primer building on a language already learned; it assists in the growth and unfolding of that language itself" (26). Orff Schulwerk places the child hand-in-hand with the teacher at the center of the curriculum and all classroom activities.

My exposure to and eventual embracing of the Schulwerk gave me the desire to create an environment of music making that was ongoing and ever-changing, with lesson designs that left room for student input. Schulwerk gave me the resources needed to teach the musical concepts in an elemental way with which I was comfortable and that clearly changed the dynamics of my teaching. These concepts, vital to the total music education of the child, are rhythm, pitch, harmony, dynamics, and tone color; and are demonstrated in speech, movement, singing, dancing, the playing of instruments, and improvisation. It is the latter that brings delight, self-esteem, ownership of work, and clear logical thinking to the students. They find their inner creative power and learn to make choices such as: which instrumental sound—wood, metal, or string—to use; whether sound or silence is best in a particular space of the music; whether to perform fast or slow; and what instrument could be used to provide the texture to show how the students feels. And they take risks by making music in solo and ensemble settings, playing in front of peers, and performing in front of a broader audience.

As I grew and changed as a teacher, I was delighted to see corresponding growth and change in my students. Instead of watching passive listeners, I saw the joy of discovery transforming children at work.

The first few years that I spent in this school system also exposed me to the philosophies of Dr. Elliot Tocci, a principal who was always looking out, looking forward, and looking around, making sure that all teachers were involved in the total education of the students. In support of this philosophy, he encouraged teacher development of the curriculum, the replacement of the traditional textbook with teacher- and student-selected resources, and the involvement and integration of all programs. Thus, the teacher-developed social studies curriculum came to include four schoolwide units with culminating activities, rotating on a five-year cycle, in which the music class played an equally important role.

I have always felt that the content and concepts of the music curriculum lend themselves naturally to learning anything, and I welcomed the opportunity to be part of this. My task became how to integrate the teaching of the elements of music through Orff-Schulwerk with other areas of learning. It was the success of the process of implementing this integration in social studies that led to the activities witnessed by the classroom visitor.

Five years before that, as we first began a unit on the Renaissance, the fifth-grade students and I researched and discussed the dances of the period. The students were drawn to the Morris and Sword Dances because of the elemental choreography, costuming, instrumental accompaniment, and their use in the culture. I had clear expectations and plans for this unit and explained them to the students. They began work the next week by sharing their researched information on the background of these dances and then voted on the one dance they would prepare. We worked together at learning the sequence of steps, using borrowed yardsticks for the swords. I had already decided to get some wood cut at a local store and paint the swords at home. All was going as I planned.

During one of our music classes, Marty reminded us that his brother, Ricky, was in the woodshop class at the high school and could probably make swords for us. A fast mental tap dance later, I thought, "I know the shop teacher, the high school's next door, Marty is so excited, everybody wants to do it, I won't have to do this alone." Soon we were writing a letter to the shop teacher asking if this was possible. When his positive reply came, the class was thrilled. The shop students would provide the swords for the dance. We set about taking measurements for the length, width, and thickness desired, and included a student drawing of the shape of the hilt. Sandy wished out loud that she could see the swords being made. A week later, we walked over to the high school to watch the students make the swords. With the smell of freshly cut wood and a cloud of sawdust around us, we walked back to music class, the proud owners of twelve new swords. Abby thought we should paint and decorate them with designs she had found in a book on the art of the Renaissance.

The next couple of weeks were full of drawing personal design choices, painting, dancing, and writing an explanation of the dance for narration. What had started as a plan on my part to expose the students to music and dance of the period ended up as research, writing, making artistic choices, using math to figure dimensions, dancing, playing instruments, and presenting a visual wonder with the performance of the Star Dance at the school's culminating activity. I had no idea when we started that we would arrive at this place, but by being open to all possibilities, by listening to and valuing the students' ideas, and by watching the project become theirs, I found that it was indeed a wonderful place to be.

We had succeeded in integrating the content curricula, music and social studies, in ways that exceeded my original hopes. In the previous two months, we had learned a lot about the Renaissance and its culture, we were in harmony with the students' regular classroom activities and content, and we had preserved the integrity of the music curriculum through which rhythm, pitch, harmony, dynamics, and tone color are demonstrated in speech, movement, singing, dancing, the playing of instruments, and improvisation. We had more than fulfilled the spirit of Orff Schulwerk by improvising at many levels, making choices, and working together. The students' improvisation took us far beyond my original outline, placed us side-by-side, and brought the two curricula into unison.

Following the social studies curriculum cycle, we returned to the Renaissance unit five years later. The students in fifth grade had been in kindergarten when they had seen the Star Dance first performed at the school's culminating activity. Their memories of this event were drawn upon in preparation for their involvement in the schoolwide gathering to share the studies of the Renaissance once again. It was because of one of these discussions that we found ourselves turning off the main road of prepared plans and venturing onto an uncharted path led by a few students. By this time, I had come to expect and welcome students taking the lead, offering both positive and negative suggestions, speaking frankly, and generating curriculum.

Caleb, who was uncomfortable expressing himself in any form of movement, had been having a difficult time focusing on anything until he saw the pictures I had brought in that depicted the lifestyles and occupations of the period. He was enthralled with a knight and let us all know that surely this man wouldn't care about dancing. Joey agreed as he chose the picture of a yeoman in full regalia. Soon others were selecting a print—a baker, a lawyer, a judge, a moneylender, a priest, a farmer, a teacher, a student—and began a discussion on who would be interested in sword dancing and why. I sat back and watched them begin to understand this period of time in their own way as they became familiar with its arts. After a while, they had discussed how each of the characters might have been affected by such a rite.

Marin asked if she could make a drawing of her chosen print and find similar costuming to wear at the culminating event. This idea appealed to the others. By the end of the class, they had decided to create large, colorful drawings to display as part of the audience that would watch their dance. I began to get that wonderful feeling of "Here we go . . ." that so often happens when the students generate new ways to learn about what can all too often become the same old thing—for students and teacher.

There really is a place for every child of every ability in every curriculum. When the teacher listens to the learning going on and provides an atmosphere of trust and acceptance, each student finds ownership of the content and, through that ownership, develops self-esteem. Improvisation is a key to the development of inner creative power and frees learners to make content their own.

The day the visitor entered the music class, the group reading the step directions to the dance were also studying form and movement. The students painting the wooden swords that would be used in the dance were also listening to the tone color of the music coming from the cassette player. The students drawing and coloring characters were singing the melody of the sword dance. And the group gathering the instruments that would be played to accompany the dancers would soon be exploring the rhythm of the dance. Everyone was engaged not only in social studies work but also in the Schulwerk.

Carl Orff likens the growth of curriculum to growth in nature: "Whenever I plant a tree, I never know how big it will be . . . some trees stay small, others grow very tall. It all depends on the quality of the earth, sunshine and other factors that have to work together" (In Frazee 1985, 5). Schulwerk and the supportive climate of my school environment were the factors that led to my own growth as a teacher and to the growth of my integrated curriculum. Through that special combination, I continually rediscover the curriculum hand-in-hand with my students.

As for Assessment

In my music classes, skills are measured by observing participation, both in the classroom and in performance. The grasp of concepts is measured by evaluating worksheets created each year. Musical understanding is measured by noticing participation in activities that use abstract thinking, and by affording numerous opportunities to the students to become thinkers, choosers, and riskers.

Value is placed on individual achievement with the use of a self-evaluation form.

Portfolios are kept, and students may select copies of audio- and/or videotapes made in class or in concert, pictures, programs, original music, manuscripts, poems, press articles, and so on, to incorporate in their portfolios. Student-written reflections are included in the student portfolio, in the performing group portfolio, and/or are shared with others.

The overall content/achievement standards are in the process of conforming to the grouping for the National Assessment of Educational Process: creation and performance, cultural and historical context, nature and value of music.

References

Frazee, Jane. 1985. "Notes from a visit with Carl Orff, January 19, 1977." In Isabel McNeil Carley, ed. *Orff Re-Echoes, Books II: Selections from the Orff Echo and the Supplements, Vols. IX–XV, 1976–1983*. Cleveland, OH: American Orff-Schulwerk Association.

Frazee, Jane, with Kent Kreuter. 1987. *Discovering Orff: A Curriculum for Music Teachers*. New York: Schott Music Corp.

Walter, Arnold. 1985. "Meditation on Method." In Isabel McNeil Carley, ed. *Orff Re-Echoes, Book II: Selections from the Orff Echo and the Supplements, Vols. IX–XV, 1976–1983*. Cleveland, OH: American Orff-Schulwerk Association.

Pat Reflects—

I've known Linda for twenty years now, as a friend and, for almost all of those years, as her colleague-in-teaching, just down the hall from each other, but I never fully appreciated her philosophy until she wrote this chapter. It's amazing to me that it could be so, but I shouldn't be surprised. Schools are, after all, places of closed doors—a lot of them—and knowing someone personally and professionally does not guarantee full understanding of one another's philosophies. I always knew that the values underpinning Linda's music program were similar to those I held, but I was interested by aspects of Carl Orff's ideas.

When I observed Linda's students practicing and performing, I could see that demonstration and active participation were central to the philosophy. What I have learned now is the importance of the role of improvisation in Orff Schulwerk, in that it brings "delight, self-esteem, ownership of work, and clear logical thinking." This emphasis on improvisation goes to the heart of a generative curriculum. Through improvisation, Orff believed, children would develop inner creativity and refine choice making. Concurrently, it is improvisation and the freedom to vary from a planned path that permits the evolution of a curriculum-in-progress, that permits students in the classroom to share in the power and decision making, to develop, as Orff says, their own creativity. I was delighted to find such compatibility in philosophies. I had never thought of describing the course of a generative curriculum as being influenced by improvisation, but I see it now.

Likewise, Linda, as a participant in Orff Schulwerk, reports collaborating with her students on an approach to learning and debating with them the choices to be made in the paths of curriculum open to the class. In this, the beliefs of Orff parallel the beliefs of whole language and optimal conditions of learning, placing learners in opportunities of use and responsibility, providing demonstrations and response, and readily accepting approximations in practice, performance, and improvisation.

Central to both philosophies is the importance of learners' engagement with topics at hand and immersion in what is to be learned. Linda "sits back," relishing the feeling of "Here we go," as students dive into the Middle Ages and all learners are involved. She says, "There really is a place for every child of every ability in every curriculum."

I also was unaware of the natural connection between Orff Schulwerk and social studies, captured in the relating of children's knowledge of their own heritage, "as it is found in nursery rhymes, folks songs, and dances," as a starting point for musical exploration. This link to the literature of the child's own life and to the culture as conveyed through song and dance is an emphasis that should be more fully integrated into the standing social studies curriculum.

As a child, I studied music separate from school, through piano lessons and music theory classes at a nearby school of music. I don't remember having music in school. Probably it took the form of learning patriotic songs as part of daily exercises. That history seems to have led me to thinking of music as something studied separately, with its own set of beliefs, philosophies, and practices. Even though I taught all those years with Linda and we collaborated on social studies and music several times each year, I somehow never made the pedagogical connection. Now, when I watch her music students create and improvise on all those xylophone-like instruments, I'll be an informed viewer. And I'll especially think of Carl Orff describing pedagogy like a river with principles that are constantly rediscovered. I'll appreciate even more Linda's observation that she finds that she continually rediscovers the curriculum "hand-in-hand with [her] students."

About Jane Rowe

Jane recalls hating social studies as a student, and so she came to teaching determined to make it better. Originally trained as an art teacher, Jane began regular, graded classroom teaching with what she describes as a "traditional" stance. In a school that at the time used no textbooks and had a mission to infuse critical and creative thinking in all subject areas, Jane became the chair of the social studies curriculum committee. Curricula in all areas were slowly being developed by teachers in the school, and Jane began to envision a new view of classroom life, centering around social studies. She feels this work greatly influenced her present thinking.

She describes the school environment at that time as "rich and fertile," one that supported her change process. It was, she says, "an environment that was competitive in a positive way, with teachers collaborating—the kind of environment that inspires you."

She did coursework at the University of Massachusetts at Boston, earning a master's degree in Critical and Creative Thinking. In her thesis she developed a working framework for infusing critical thinking across the curriculum. This moved her own growth process forward. She began consulting and working with teachers and found that this was valuable in that it "asked all the questions" and she had to think about the answers and problem solve. She also served as a consultant and devoted a great deal of her time to working with the Massachusetts Department of Education in developing authentic assessment in social studies with critical thinking as a base. She published an account of her school's work with social studies in Educational Leadership *(November 1990), in an article entitled "Learning to Teach Thinking: One School's Story."*

Jane is the mother of two daughters, and she feels this has greatly influenced her teaching style. "Being a mother," she says, "I knew what I wanted for my own kids." She feels now that she is mother first, even in the classroom, and thinks a lot about the fact that "a year for a child is such a big difference."

Leaving the art room and going into the classroom gave Jane time, she says, to find ways to make a difference in the lives of children. She credits Dr. Robert Swartz of University of Massachusetts and Dr. Wanda Teays, who Jane worked with in the Critical and Creative Thinking Program, for teaching her and helping her grow and change.

Here in her chapter, we see the influence of a teacher-developed curriculum with infused critical thinking as the core—a program that promotes student decision making and thoughtful actions.

CHAPTER EIGHT

Critical Thinking and Social Studies in the Fifth Grade

Jane Rowe

When my students arrive in the classroom on the first day of school, they are surprised to find the desks and chairs not lined up in a neat and orderly fashion, but rather piled up along the wall with (bigger surprise) price tags on them, ranging from "$12.00 per week" to "$24.00 per week." Some of these desks and chairs are shiny and fairly new, while others have obviously seen better days, and each piece of furniture is priced accordingly.

In a class meeting necessarily conducted on the floor, the system is explained: during fifth grade, the students would be expected to "pay" for things; in turn, they would be "paid" for their work at an hourly wage, with opportunities to earn extra "money." Students are "paid" in a classroom script and in tokens. The tokens are small, colored glass globs given to me by my father, from his earlier period of interest in stained-glass work. (No elementary school teacher ever turns down any offer of anything with even remotely interesting possibilities. These pieces looked like jewels, something wonderful just to have.)

Friday is payday. Students fill out budget worksheets with information from the previous week to determine their pay. Such calculations are an integral part of the math program in our class. I am the banker in the beginning, but ultimately this becomes a class job that students apply for and are paid for. Once a student has settled accounts with the banker, he or she is eligible to visit the Company Store to purchase school supplies or snacks.

The economic system in my classroom has evolved gradually over several years. Though there are variations to this program every year to accommodate each current situation, with some aspects changed to fit the curriculum and some generated by the students themselves, basically the system is structured much the same from year to year. Students arrive, find price tags on the desks and chairs, and roll into

115

a year-long simulation that is integrated with the regular curriculum in a number of ways. As with any generative curriculum, these changes may be student initiated, teacher supported, or simply spontaneous. Markets develop some years, with students selling one another items from home. On occasion, indoor recess takes on the appearance of a giant yard sale or flea market. Checking accounts, savings accounts, various insurances, and credit have been introduced at the request of students in some years. There are occasional "investment opportunities" tied to academic domains that allow students to make—or lose—money. Once the basic system components are in place, it works best if we simply "go with the flow," being careful not to get in too deep too quickly so that program management does not become impossible.

There is much math involved in this system, with students learning and applying proficiency in computation, calculator employment, and, eventually, computer spreadsheet skills. When the structure of the classroom economy is established, it also becomes integrated into the regular academic curricula in areas other than math.

For instance, while working through a unit on the American Revolution, students were trying to understand that life was not as cut and dried politically during this period as old textbooks might have us believe, with all of the reasonable people being patriots, and any supporter of English rule being a "bad guy." Each student had been given an identity of a fictional character from this period of colonial America, along with extensive background information about the character's family, occupation, connections, and general living situation. During the course of the study, students were provided with various experiences to help them to understand opposing viewpoints. Some of these experiences were intimately tied to the classroom economic system.

For example, one Monday morning many students opened their desks to find boxes inside. These intruders ranged in size and shape from tie and jewelry boxes to shirt boxes and shoe boxes. Each was tied up tightly with a string and accompanied by a reproduction of a notice announcing the quartering of British soldiers in private homes. There was a small hole in the top corner of each box and a number indicating how many soldiers would be quartered. Students who were so unlucky as to be forced to house "soldiers" in their desks not only had to undergo the more crowded conditions in their "homes" and the general indignity of having these new conditions thrust upon them, but they were also required to "feed" each soldier a token a day. This lesson hit home hard with all students, even those who had been fortunate enough, for whatever reasons, to escape this fate. They developed a personal understanding of the colonists' reactions to this situation and an appreciation for the inclusion of the third amendment to the Constitution forbidding the quartering of soldiers in private homes.

Another time, during a study of America's Westward Expansion, students entered a simulation in which they made the traditional westward trek. They planned the trip and "packed their wagons," all purchases being made from and limited by their personal "savings."

Some entire units of study are designed around the classroom economic system. For example, our study of the Industrial Revolution began with a sign advertising a sale of stock certificates to eligible individuals. Students owning stock could earn dividends. For one budding capitalist, this advertisement posed a golden opportunity: Seth immediately came to me with a thousand dollars in cash and tokens and announced that he wished to buy twenty shares of stock in GFES Enterprises—the perennial title for our classroom economic undertakings, Grade Five Economic System.

I hadn't thought that Seth had accumulated so many assets, but I took his money, gave him a receipt, and returned to school the following day with two stock certificates bearing his name. It turned out that Seth *hadn't* had that much money. However, he did have the business acumen to recognize an opportunity, and had quickly arranged several loans from classmates who hadn't enough capital of their own to invest in the stock market but welcomed the opportunity to earn interest on their smaller savings. Four students in all made stock purchases. Lisa and Jessup had enough capital of their own to make the purchases, and Maria had convinced others to pool their money in her name.

Students listened carefully to the rules of the game, a fairly complicated set of contingencies detailing the buying and selling and rental of properties as well as the stock investments. A number of students who saw exciting money-making possibilities as landlords quickly invested in "real estate"—desks and chairs. Students engaged in interesting informal discussions, debating the wisdom of purchasing one's own desk versus becoming a "landlord," renting desks to others. A major change in the economic system occurred during these Industrial Revolution studies. No longer were students paid for their time at an hourly wage; now they did "piecework" and were paid only for the work that they actually produced.

During this time, problems began to develop. Seth had clearly overextended himself. He had developed fancy tastes and had been tempted by the purchase of some status symbols for his new desk. Of course, this new address carried a fancy rent as well, and having spent all of his savings plus borrowed money to purchase his stock, Seth was in trouble. He finally realized that the only way out of his troubles was to liquidate his assets, namely his stocks.

As had been explained to the class at the beginning of the unit, stock could be auctioned off if a student wished to sell and other students were willing to buy. However, the selling price affected the value of everyone else's stock. I had promised to buy back all shares of stock at the conclusion of the unit at the most recent selling price. Students who did not yet own stock saw an opportunity to pick up some shares cheap. As the announced time for the auction drew near, there was a flurry of activity, with students negotiating to borrow funds from one another to make the purchase individually or to form trusts to make the purchase jointly. Meanwhile, the stockholders banded together, trying to drive up the price of the stock. Marty was the high bidder on Seth's stock at $350.00 for ten shares. In the uproar of the bidding she had, however, bid more cash than she actually possessed, but a friend loaned her the needed twenty-three dollars.

Another problem arose when Tina got sick—not just a one-day sort of cold, but a full-blown case of the flu that kept her out of school for a week and a half. Tina grew frantic about finding enough money to pay her rent. She was too ill to do her work.

The experience was realistic, and everyone learned from it. They had read books such as *Lyddie* (Patterson 1991), *A Family Apart* (Nixon 1987), *Immigrant Kids* (Freedman 1980), and *Tenement Writer* (Sonder 1993), historical fiction and nonfiction accounts of people being down and out during this historical period, at a time before social reforms had become commonplace. Now, Tina's situation helped them to understand how circumstances beyond one's control could overwhelm a person.

There was a major class discussion about this. Many students felt that the situation was unfair because Tina had really been sick. Others pointed out that this was the kind of thing that really happened, citing Betsy's case in *Lyddie*. Sandy asked, "Why doesn't Tina just go on welfare?" and it had to be explained that the welfare system hadn't yet been established in U.S. history.

Tina and I had some private talks about this situation, and of course my protective instincts made me want to "rescue" her. I involved her mother in this decision, and it was a difficult time for us all. It couldn't have been much more real, a true test of a generative curriculum. I decided to try to let the situation run its course, give Tina my moral support, and hope for the best.

The whole experience motivated Tina to become active in trying to form a union. Unfortunately, the activists never were able to summon enough support to take any action. The eight weeks spent on this unit just weren't quite long enough to allow the course of events to go full swing.

However, the culminating activity for this unit was an anthology of historical fiction, stories based upon the students' personal experiences within the classroom, as well as their research, and many of the stories, including those authored by the stockholders, ended with social and legal reform. Some were satires, with animals characterizing the various roles within our classroom simulation. Others were more literal tales simply describing personal experiences.

The experience also spawned numerous class discussions about the role of government, perceptions of the need for government interference, workers' rights, socialist reform, and more. While much information came from their reading or from films, every student had a strong opinion based upon a personal point of view gained during the simulation experience. Thus, students were actively involved, not only in the simulation activities, but also in the reflective process that assimilated history with personal experience. These activities promoted a much greater understanding of the issues than if we simply had "studied" them in a more traditional approach.

At the culmination of our studies of the Industrial Revolution, stock shares were cashed in for $35.00 per share. Investors performed calculations to determine how they actually had made out financially, balancing the dividends earned against their capital losses. Could they have done better investing in real estate rather than stock? There was much reflection regarding that point. It was a good question to think about, they realized, but one without a definitive answer considering all of the variables.

Students had learned a great deal about economics, about the Industrial Revolution, and about the concept of point of view. An authors' party to celebrate the publication of our stories was attended by a large group of relatives and friends; students dressed in period costumes to read their stories (or excerpts in the case of very long works) and eagerly collected one another's autographs on their own copies of the anthology. GFES Enterprises bought back Tina's desk, to her great relief, and furniture was rearranged once again to accommodate new needs and a new unit of study. Although most of the students begged to continue "living in the Industrial Revolution," it was time to move on to Brazil, with a new set of investment opportunities.

Each June, as the year ends, after the final bell rings and the last student leaves the room for the last time, I sit and reflect amidst the clutter of spent tokens and currency. Unable to resist, I make the rounds of desks to sneak a peek at the letters left for next year's class:

> Dear Person Who Will Be Sitting in My Desk Next Year,
>
> I hope that you like this desk. It has been a good desk. It squeaks but I like it anyway . . . I am leaving my lucky token for you. James left it for me last year and it has been good luck. I hope it works for you too. Blue tokens are the best. Good luck in fifth grade.
>
> Sincerely,
>
>
> *Jenny*

As for Assessment

Assessment in this classroom is a combination of traditional and innovative approaches. Students are occasionally given written quizzes or tests in a given subject area. There are also performance checklists, which attempt to quantify and/or qualify such things as participation in class discussion or contribution to a group effort. Reports or formal presentations are scored with regard to criteria given to students in advance of the assignment. (Sometimes these criteria are established solely by the teacher; other times the students have input. This usually depends upon the time of the year and the students' cumulative experience.) Occasionally, the entire class fills out individual scorecards regarding their perception of the degree to which a performance meets the stated criteria. Student critiques are sometimes employed. Peer feedback is for the benefit of the student performing, not for the teacher.

A portfolio is maintained for each student. This holds a variety of work, some important, some mundane, some teacher-selected, some student-selected. Work that is three-dimensional or of a performance nature is recorded on audio- or videotapes—each child has both. Students are encouraged to take the tapes home to view with parents and to reflect on an individual project or performance as well as upon their progress over time. Students' reflections upon their work is an important component of the portfolio.

Even though a unit such as the Industrial Revolution simulation is generative to a great degree, there is always some method to my madness before beginning the unit, and some specific goals that are to be achieved. The path to these goals lies between the "situation" that

Critical Thinking and Social Studies in the Fifth Grade

.... 121

students are given initially (in this case, the opportunity to buy stock; the roles of capitalist or worker, and the culminating activity (in this case, a piece of writing, specifically, a work of historical fiction synthesizing learned concepts and content in the social studies with writing and word processing skills). Early on, students were told about the writing project and given the parameters as well as the criteria upon which the story and their social studies performance would be assessed.

Upon completion of a unit, students are given clean copies of the criteria score sheets (points indicating the relative weight/importance given to different facets of their work). They reflect independently upon their success in meeting each criterion and score themselves accordingly. I use identical sheets to score each student's performance myself. Soon afterward, the students and I sit in short individual conferences to compare the results. Almost always our scores are virtually the same in each category. Whenever there is a discrepancy we discuss it. The student has the opportunity to persuade me to change my opinion, and I can explain to the student my reasons for a different score.

These sheets also contain written student reflections and teacher comments. They are attached to the final project (including all drafts) and become a part of each student's permanent portfolio. The final "score" becomes a major basis for the report card grade, and the work in the portfolio becomes the basis for discussing the grade with parents at the report card conference. Ultimately, the contents of these portfolios are used by the students for their exit-exhibitions at the end of the sixth grade, in which all students make presentations demonstrating what and how they have learned in their elementary school experiences.

References

Freedman, Russell. 1980. *Immigrant Kids*. New York: Scholastic, Inc.

Nixon, Joan Lowery. 1987. *A Family Apart*. New York: Bantam Books.

Patterson, Katherine. 1991. *Lyddie*. New York: The Trumpet Club.

Sonder, Ben. 1993. *The Tenement Writer: An Immigrant's Story*. New York: Steck-Vaughn Co.

Pat Reflects—

Whenever I read this account, I am struck by the power of engaging students in real-life, ongoing interactions. As we work closely to re-create the life of the times, we must create a realistic picture of how life was. One of the criticisms I share of traditional textbooks is the hasty way in which they gloss over problems and personal repercussions in historical times. It is hard for anyone to understand some of the great reforms that we today enjoy without a clear view of the conditions that provoked them.

Often re-creating the life of the times has been reserved for older students, up into high school, on the grounds that younger children perhaps shouldn't know too much that is often disturbing. But modern teachers don't all share this view, and even first-grade teachers some-times take on deep and troubling subjects such as war and peace as thematic units with their students. The field of process writing is currently being criticized in some quarters for encouraging children to write "any old thing" in the name of writing every day—for not presenting children with meaningful topics to write about that are relevant to the modern world they live in. Determining the proper subject matter for children is an argument going far back into our educational history.

The key to this issue, it seems to me, is the nature of the environment we as teachers establish around the studies at hand. Of central importance is the respect we show for our students and their learning and the respect we engender in them for us and for each other. Equally important is the secure and supportive environment we provide and the helping hand we supply. At no time in this classroom, we say to students, will your worth and self-esteem be sacrificed for the sake of learning. When you are in this room, you are safe, secure, and well-supported, and I am always here to help.

I have probably learned more about social studies from Jane Rowe than from almost any other person. Jane and I have done workshops together, taught courses together, and argued endlessly over the details of social studies and literacy.

Jane describes herself as a teacher of critical thinking, and her extensive background in that field supports her. She promotes a critical thinking philosophy infused into a base of social studies. Most importantly, Jane believes in authentic learning. She engages her students in simulations based in social studies and literacy in order to to help them understand different times, places, and people. The work that she and the students do in the classroom is done because it is necessary to advance a common cause, not because the teacher needs something to correct.

The conditions of optimal learning are in place in Jane's classroom. Jane strongly believes in *immersion*. She believes that in order to truly understand a time or a place, people have to become part of it and experience it for themselves. For much of the school day, she and her students are immersed in a simulation, seeking to understand, for example, a particular period of time, like the Industrial Revolution in the United States. There is ongoing opportunity and encouragement for *use* of previously learned skills and strategies, and of newfound abilities, as her students read and write in character about an experience they're having. While simulation activities are designed so that they are *appropriate* for all students, no matter what their present level of performance, there is a high level of *expectation*, and students are encouraged to challenge themselves by taking *responsibility* to go beyond what they have expected of themselves in the past. This sometimes manifests itself as students who have not previously seen themselves as readers begin to read for a purpose, or as students who are not comfortable with their own writing process feel compelled to write letters to next year's students, advising them about the experiences they will have: "Dear Person Who will Be Sitting in My Desk Next Year, This is a good desk but it squeeks when you open it. It is not to expensive. The chip in the corner happened when Jason tipped his chair and knocked my desk over to."

Jane and students *demonstrate* new concepts, skills, strategies, and content to be learned, and students, as they *use* all this in daily classwork, receive *response* both from Jane and from each other. There is a lot of talk in Jane's classroom. *Approximations* are accepted, indeed welcomed, especially from students who have a history of worrying about their performance, while conventional forms are continually demonstrated and modeled. The ongoing simulations are designed to promote *engagement* on the part of all students and teacher alike. Jane and her students "dwell in the times" of the social studies topic at hand.

Jane's classroom is also literature-based. Books are used to introduce and explore topics in social studies. Since students in the simulations are "living in the times," the stories in the books take on new and relevant meaning. These meanings are often later translated into children's written stories, which become more authentic because students have had real, concrete experiences to relate to, and have read and discussed others' fictional accounts.

There is a lot of metacognitive talk, especially around problem solving and decision making, in Jane's classroom. This is characteristic of a curriculum with infused critical thinking. On her wall is a large, generic, problem-solving model, showing the different stages of the process. Often she and her students stop to talk about where they are in the problem-solving or decision-making process, especially as it relates to their current simulation in social studies. These talks are extensive and in-depth and sometimes continue over several days. Often they spend time filling in the problem-solving model to track their progress in this problem-based curriculum. Students graduating from her room are quite cognizant of the various stages of their own process and are adept at discussing their status and progress in thinking and learning. This ability to talk about one's own process, to reflect metacognitively, is the most powerful aspect of infused critical thinking and marks people who have been in such a program.

Jane's classroom also works within a generative curriculum. She sets up the simulations initially, providing rules and guidelines for what become "life games" for her students. Then she becomes one of the players, too, while the life of the simulation unfolds. Its path is directed by the choices made by the students and teacher, and the successes and problems are outcomes of the situation and of the decisions made by the participants. The culminating activity may be known in advance, such as an anthology of student writing, or a schoolwide fair representing the time or place being studied. But how the class gets there, and the individual lives that are constructed on the way, are the direct result of the actions of the students and teachers within the story created within the simulation.

This personal involvement in the story contrasts with a form of teaching social studies known as "the Scottish Storyline." In role playing and simulations, participants are directly involved with the roles they create and play. In Scottish Storyline, participants work with models of the character they are creating. I learned about this methodology, widely used to teach social studies to children in Europe, from Steve Bell of Jordanhill College in Glasgow, Scotland, and from Ian Bell, Director of Curriculum and Evaluation at the Scottish Consultative Council on the Curriculum. It is gaining favor in this country partly through the writing and presentations of Margit McGuire (1991), past president of the National Council of Social Studies. Scottish Storyline combines art, story, and social studies through the production by children of large murals, which become the setting for the story, and the creation of characters, rather like paper dolls, through which the story is developed. The path of the curriculum evolves through the development of key questions related to the curricular theme. It is a generative curriculum, reflecting the decisions made by the students whose lives are being represented by the paper figurines. The rationale behind the development of these paper figures is to set the children one step removed from the story they are creating, to let them act *on*, rather than *in*, the story.

I bring this philosophy and methodology to the readers' attention because, as we see in Jane's account, developing role playing experiences to be lived by children in classrooms produces great insight on their part about the life of the times and also produces the possibility of students learning sadder lessons about the times they are studying.

Like Jane, I am committed to role playing and simulations. Without them, I would miss the personal involvement, the element of pretend, the power of imagination. Sometimes, as Jane demonstrates, we engage students in quite real, day-to-day experiences, replicating as closely as we can the concepts and activities being studied. One of my favorite and, I think, most effective, mini, true-to-life simulations occurred one year when my sixth graders and I were preparing to gather information about the recycling effort in preparation for taking part in a schoolwide mock town meeting to consider a referendum on recycling, which was a real issue for the town that year. Although my students knew a lot about taking out the garbage, I thought that they might not understand so well why garbage is such a problem in our modern world. So I secretly arranged with Sam, the custodian who supervised the lunch clean-up, that he would refuse to accept the after-lunch trays from my sixth graders. He was a willing participant. This simulation left my students with some very realistic garbage, which they showed me, asking, "What do we do now?" I said they'd have to bring it back to the room until we could find a solution for this problem. Back in the room with our trays of trash—because Sam didn't accept mine, either—we discussed options. Minnie finally went to see Sam to get some big garbage bags. The students decided to store their refuse in the greenhouse attached to the classroom—the classroom equivalent of "throwing it over the hill," a common solution in older times.

We did this for two days, and then it was the weekend. When we returned on Monday, we had a problem. It being May, the garbage had begun to make itself known, and ants had found the bags. There the simulation ended—but with much discussion. Sam came with the truck and took away the offending garbage bags. My students said, "Mrs. Cordeiro . . ." in that tone they used when they knew that I had been up to something, and we sat for a long time, talking about recycling. Students recognized that if Sam had not come, they would have had to come up with an immediate solution. Some of them knew about composting because their families practiced it. We talked about options for families and options for towns, and when we launched into our study of the choices the town had to make for their own future as local citizens, my students spoke with the voices of those who really know.

Simulations offer the best opportunities to engage learners personally in problems and concepts at hand. I continue to believe that we do little in schools that is more powerful than to give all learners, including ourselves, a chance to "walk in the life of the times."

References

McGuire, Margit. 1991. "Conceptual Learning in the Primary Grades: the Storyline Strategy." In *Social Studies and the Young Learner* 3:6–9.

Generating and Adapting Curriculum: Learning from Each Other

Pat Cordeiro

One of the most amazing things about a school is the variety of relationships that are possible within its walls. Another is how secluded the interactions really are. Garth Boomer et al. (1992) observe that ". . . by and large, teaching acts are shockingly private and undocumented" (ix). These authors call for research that will accumulate records of practice about "the infinitely complex business of teaching" (ix).

These quotes struck me as I read them because I suddenly realized that I know a great deal more about the teachers on the previous pages than I ever did about the teachers down the hall, or about the successes in my colleague Helen's classroom next door. Similarly, I know more about Bobbi Fisher's (1991) classroom from her book, or Nancie Atwell's (1987) classroom from hers, or Linda Rief's (1992) from hers—their hopes and dreams, their problems—than I ever knew about the teachers in the primary wing around the corner.

Schools are curious places. Student teachers report observations that come as no surprise: There are some teachers out there who have an "open door" policy, and there are some teachers who, as college students put it, would rather "cut off their right arm than share with you their 'secrets' for teaching." There are some who have "*twelve boxes of 'stuff*" that they use when they teach *Lyddie* [Patterson 1991], and you better not use it at your grade level . . ."

But the fact of the matter is, schools are greatly enhanced when there is collaboration, sharing, and cooperation between teachers. Teachers in this volume benefited from collaboration and discussion with colleagues about what they wanted to do and how they might adapt their plans to fit those of the students. And this collaboration went beyond serving on and chairing committees that determined language and social studies policies within a school.

One of the notable things about the teachers in this volume is their openness about themselves, their change process, their classrooms, and their hopes and dreams. Certainly this must be a factor in the great distances they report having traveled in their growth as teachers.

All of them give workshops for other teachers. Somewhere during their careers, the opportunity to tell others about what was going on in their classrooms presented itself, and they seized the opportunity. Teachers who haven't yet given workshops may be thinking, "Well, that's for them—they have something important to say." But I don't think any of us felt that our programs were particularly special or important when we first started sharing them with teachers. Many of us simply felt that we *had to talk to somebody* about what we were doing, get some feedback, and share with others. And, as so many authors in this volume report, it was through sharing with others that their own ideas continued to grow. As they thought hard about how to convey their own classroom to other teachers, through talking and writing, they found themselves thinking very hard about their own learning and teaching. So one thing began to feed the other until the growth process for them became circular—the more they shared, the more they had to share.

For teachers reading this book who are interested in making changes, I think this sense of community and sharing with other teachers is one of the key factors and a beginning point for many of us. Teachers making change seek out other teachers who are making change, through speaker events, through organizations, through visiting other schools, and through reading professional books. Within the evolution of the whole language movement, teachers shared with each other through what became known as TAWL (Teachers Applying Whole Language) groups. Often these were small get-togethers in a member's living room, with people talking about what they were doing, their hopes and dreams, and supporting each other in change and growth. These grassroots informal meetings have been essential for teachers who might be the only ones in their school trying out new ideas and breaking away from textbooks and worksheets. Some TAWL groups have since evolved into study groups, with teachers directing their own learning. These self-selected "in-service workshops" are often occasions for discussing a professional book that all the members are reading, or a time for discussing a presentation that everyone attended.

Adapting Programs

The programs in this book are presented as having been tried at certain grades, but are certainly adaptable to different grade levels. I give a workshop for teachers about simulations I have done with sixth graders. These are excursions into literacy and social studies, and I always bill the workshop as being about upper elementary work. What always amazes me are the numbers of primary, middle school, high school, and college teachers who attend this workshop, and the results of their implementation of the ideas. I have had positive feedback on the "transferability" of ideas from many, many grade levels, from first grade, to higher education to special education.

How do teachers go about doing this? I think they do exactly what I did when I first started. I entered my classroom with an idea, with the beginning of a plan, with the first activity in a sequence of activities, and probably with a general idea of how the unit of study would wind up—a culminating activity idea—and then I listened to my students— and to myself. One of the most powerful things about a generative curriculum is that it gives a central place to teachers' and students' intuition and insight.

I see common elements in these programs that apply across classrooms and across grades. The first is a commitment to providing optimal conditions of learning. In all of these descriptions, students and teacher are immersed in the work to be done, often on a full-time basis, carrying over several days or more. This immersion carries with it many opportunities for the use of various tools, processes, skills, strategies, and content, together with a firm responsibility placed on each and every learner to take part and make the subject one's own. Students and teachers alike accept each others' approximations and give appropriate and helpful responses to enable all to create their own versions of what has been demonstrated. All are expected to be able to participate, and a variety of ways to engage with topics are provided. In all of these classroom descriptions, learning is authentic and appropriate, that is, what is done by teacher and students has a larger purpose than fulfilling a teacher's mandate or completing the work listed on the board.

In all of these settings, there is a strong sense of community, supported by opportunities for interaction among participants. This community is renewed through much talk and group planning. The community often stops together and checks progress and reassesses direction, like explorers on a long trek regularly consulting map and compass.

These descriptions are marked by the sharing of process and reflection. Teachers and students alike often discuss how things are being done, how ideas and decisions were arrived at, and why one choice seems better than another. Students are encouraged and enabled to be self-reflective, considering their strengths and areas for growth. To me, this reflective talk, this application of metacognition, is one of the most striking characteristics of classrooms with generative curricula.

All of these accounts include a great deal of involvement with literacy. This includes the use of literature as a link between the past and the present, and, particularly, historical fiction as a means of bringing the lives of the people into focus for modern children. Through reading literature, learners are encouraged to write literature, to relate their own concrete learnings to more distant times and happenings through the processes of writing and storytelling. Traditionally, we have assigned this task only to older children, believing it was too hard for young children. But accounts in this book show clearly that children of all ages, in all stages of emergent writing, can use the creation of literature as a means of self-expression.

In all of these classrooms, much is made concrete. Children experience what they are reading, thinking, and talking about by means such as Sandra's classroom cabin or Judy's plays. Students in Linda's music class make and create real things to help them express their understanding of topics at hand. I have always felt that we got rid of the "kindergarten store" too early—the classroom space that might one week be a store, another week be the fire station. We all need places set aside for dreaming and imagining.

And in all of these accounts, there is an element of imagination. Participants—students and teachers alike—are free to stretch their minds, "to walk in the times," to pretend to be people living quite different lives from their own. In this climate of improvisation, in Carl Orff's terminology, generative curriculum naturally grows.

This element of imagination makes what we're learning larger than life, restoring to us that sense of elevated importance that everything had when we were six years old, when we first entered school and everything seemed so big, so important. The work I did at that age in school was grand, much better than anything I had done before. But of course that feeling quickly dwindled as school became routine, boring, and sometimes worse. My main memory of third grade is copying out all the numbers up to something like a thousand, a routine task designed to keep the third graders busy for a long, long time while the teacher attended to the fourth graders in our multi-age classroom. While the final number seemed awfully high to me, the task did not seem important, and the teacher must have worked awfully hard to invest it with some sense of worth just to get us to do it.

So for me, as school proceeded, life outside school regained the primary importance, the place where "big stuff" happened. Going to a basketball game with my father when I was in third grade become larger than life, exciting, the best thing that had ever happened. School became something to do in between the "big stuff." What the accounts described in this book do is to restore to school learning a sense of excitement, a sense of being larger than life. Children in these classrooms know that the work they do everyday is significant and makes a difference, and therefore they are invested in it.

In all of these classrooms there is interaction and talk. The traditional classroom stance, especially common in social studies instruction, of the teacher standing up, in front, talking to students who are sitting down, in silent rows, has been overturned in favor of shared talking and free movement. Ideas are tried out in public before they become cemented in learners' minds. This supports the beliefs of Vygotsky (1978), who wrote, "All the higher functions originate as actual relations between human beings" (57). Thus, thinking is done, in Vygotsky's terminology, intra-psychologically—between people—before it becomes inter-psychological—within people's minds. Learning happens best when it occurs first as interaction and then is internalized.

Finally, I am struck by recurring words in these accounts. In particular, I see the word *listen* over and over. Teachers in these accounts report that change for them is accompanied by a feature of listening, really listening, to their students. Often they seem to feel that they are listening for the first time. This stands in contrast to what is traditionally seen as the teachers' main professional asset, described in pre-service literature as "with-it-ness," the ability a teacher has to be in tune with the whole room all at once. This is certainly a great asset and allows one teacher to be aware of the movements, the progress, and the presence of many children at once. But this sense of "with-it-ness" often stands in the way of real interaction with individual students. I remember when I first began a process writing program in my classroom and initiated my first writing conferences. I was shocked when the third grader came to the end of her story and I didn't know what to ask—I couldn't remember a thing she had said. I hadn't listened at all. My sense of "with-it-ness" had prevented me from connecting, from attending, from doing the kind of listening essential to real understanding. It was quite a while before I was able to moderate this trait.

These teachers have learned how to listen and to connect with the learning going on around—and within—them. While retaining their sense of "with-it-ness," they have discovered how to do "detailed" listening, too. This in turn has allowed them to step back, consider the thoughts and ideas of the students, and reassess the curriculum and the interactions in the classroom. Then, through enlisting each other as colleagues, teachers and students have set up new patterns of dynamics for themselves.

Future Teachers of Social Studies, Literacy, and Whole Language

I give a lot of thought to how to help both preservice and teachers-in-service accomplish for themselves and their students the successes that the classrooms described in this volume enjoy. While I feel it is important that adult students in methods classes read the great theorists and master the art of teaching, I think it is essential that they continue to study the art of learning. Garth Boomer (1992), in his seminal article "Negotiating the Curriculum," points out that in the school documents he studied, "*Teaching* theory abounded" but "few departmental statements addressed learning theory" (5). Furthermore, he notes: few teachers could articulate what they assumed about learning.

> Imagine education-department curriculum guides, with no explicit learning theory, being taken by teachers with no explicit learning theory and turned into lessons for children who are not told the learning theory. Some of the best of these children then graduate to become teachers. And so on. (5)

Long after I developed the process and content of my college methods classes, I read this essay. Boomer gave voice to what I had already found to be true. As is so often the case for me, theory has followed practice and intuition.

In a methods class devoted to social studies, I am initially dismayed again and again when I ask students to talk about their memories of social studies from their elementary school days. If I am lucky, two or three out of twenty will report positive memories. Many have no memories at all, or only memories of round-robin reading of social studies texts. Two or three have bad memories. Sometimes they were humiliated when they couldn't memorize the capitals of the states, or their grade on a social studies test was publicly discussed with their name attached, but usually they were embarrassed when they were called on to read their paragraph in the textbook aloud. It's very sad.

The upshot of all of this is that most of my students have rejected social studies as something they can look forward to teaching. Many of them save this methods class until last in the series of discipline-based practicum experiences offered at the college where I teach. It's rare for me to find students who come to class excited about the prospects for getting out there and teaching social studies.

I think Garth Boomer is right on the mark: students have had a lot of talk about teaching and not enough about learning. And the learning they should start with is their own. I continue to believe that there is nothing more powerful for teachers to contemplate than the learning they underwent as children. I think we will all continue to teach as we were taught unless we carefully examine and consider our own childhood experiences.

My main goal in teaching this social studies methods course is to help students to enjoy and appreciate social studies as a living, vital force, present all around them. To do this, we start each class with what we first call "social studies trivia" and later call "everyday social studies." We discuss things we've heard or seen that seemed like social studies but we weren't really sure why. Initially, my students have a narrow view of social studies as history and map-drawing, and it's sometimes hard to get this part of the class going. I want them to realize that social studies is the life we all live, the world going on around us, the things that happen every day on our streets; and I want to bring the study of "civics" out of the ninth-grade closet and into the mainstream.

My own elementary-school students, no matter what the grade level, always had the unnerving habit of arriving in the morning excited about something that had happened. In my early years, it totally disrupted my curriculum for the day. Later, I cherished these golden opportunities. Always, those things that had happened had a connection to the world of social studies—a fire on somebody's street, an earthquake in Bolivia, a confrontation in Iran, a wandering moose lost in New England geography.

I want my college students to see *their* students' excitements—those engagements—as golden opportunities, too. And I want to give them the tools to be able to lead those natural student involvements into something larger and to connect them to the world and goals of social studies. I recognize that teachers are accountable for what happens during their days; that concern for accountability probably is responsible for more lost opportunities than anything else. So, in these college classroom discussions, we discuss news and personal events, and we "tie things down" to the goals of social studies, to readings, to theory. Sometimes the discussions of current events take a lot of time: "The Governor shot raccoons in his yard—what does that say about citizens bearing arms—what about environmental concerns—he has state troopers on guard—can anyone take the law into their own hands" and so we go.

I also have students immediately integrate literature into the study of social studies. Few have had that connection made in school. We read Eleanor Tate's (1987) *The Secret of Gumbo Grove*, a wonderful description of how a young girl researches the history of her own town and culture. We have literature discussion groups and make charts, diagrams, drawings, and graphics, and we talk about how we might use literature to augment, enhance, and centralize a social studies curriculum.

We don't use traditional college textbooks in this course. Rather, I try to provide students with fine-quality professional books that will be useful to them as teachers, ones that I know my teaching friends are reading. We've used *Small Group Learning in the Classroom* by Reid, Forrestal, and Cook (1989), a book found useful and mentioned by Douglas Barnes; and we've found that Don Graves's (1989) *Investigate Nonfiction* is relevant and informative for writing in content areas. More recently, we've also been using Karen Jorgensen's (1993) *History Workshop: Reconstructing the Past with Elementary Students*; and Michael Tunnell and Richard Ammon's (1993) *The Story of Ourselves: Teaching History Through Children's Literature*.

I ask students to choose a meaningful, personal project that relates to social studies—and that leaves it wide open. I have so very few students who have ever done anything that mattered to them personally before, something that was connected to the world of social studies, that I almost feel a moral obligation to give them the opportunity. I have received such a wonderful range of projects. Many do family histories, as my sixth graders did; some college students research places near them that they care about—the carousel at the state park, an old cemetery they've always wondered about, an old building they work in, some report "feeling like Raisin" in *The Secret of Gumbo Grove* by researching something important to them; some interview and research things they've always wondered about—the history of the Vietnam War, the Freemasons, the tragedy at Bhopal, the bridge that their uncle built. This project has been the most rewarding part of this class, and I have found that one class period is not enough for the sharing time—students are so enthusiastic, we need two class periods, or even three.

I ask them to develop a unit of study for the students they work with, building toward a culminating activity—a class sharing in the school multipurpose room of all that's been learned. They use student- and teacher-developed materials for all of this, turning to the textbook only as another resource. During the semester, I have engaged them in a mini-simulation of "Going West in America," so that they could recapture the power of imagination in their learning and teaching. Many of them continue this into their work with children.

In class we talk and interact; when we can, we sit in a circle so that we can all talk to each other. Talking and interacting is not always easy in a college classroom. Much college subject matter lends itself best to sitting, listening, and writing. College students have had a lifetime of not talking and not moving in school. Most college students I work with have spent as many as fifteen years talking to the backs of people's heads, when they have talked at all. But relating to people who are turned away is not a natural act. People relate to each other face-to-face, and only in a school setting does turning away, being backward to each other, not signal downright hostility in human relations.

We talk about the meaning of this strange school-related phenomenon, and the related implications of youngsters—and older people, too—sitting so still for so long as a school day. We try to find alternatives, both for ourselves as learners and for the students we will all work with. We move around and talk, trying out new ways of classroom interaction and new ways of making school work. Throughout, we search together for ways to bring the excitement of social studies as we are discovering it into the lives of the children we work with in schools.

Conclusions

I hope you have enjoyed this book; I have greatly enjoyed compiling the chapters by teachers that are the heart of it. I feel, in a way, that the writers of this volume and I are part of an effort to revive the great world of social studies, to rescue it from the covers of uncountable numbers of social studies textbooks, covered with dust and graffiti.

Social studies, through connections to literacy and whole language, is one of the most powerful components of the curriculum today. Only through social studies will we excite children to preserve democracy, think clearly and critically, and understand one another. Only through linking social studies to literature, reading and writing, will children—future citizens—make sense of their minds and all they absorb from day to day.

I believe that we must articulate our beliefs and histories, and take what Boomer calls "a constructively irreverent stance" toward them, challenging what we have been so that we can open up to what we can be. Everything we learn reflects our values and practices about how we learn. This book presents the compelling idea that "teachers and children may collaboratively build learning theories" (Boomer 1992,5) through generating curriculum together. I wish readers well as they explore the possibilities, adapt, change and grow new programs. As readers cultivate their own greenhouses, I hope they find, as I have, that what teachers really cultivate is progress for us all.

References

Atwell, Nancie. 1987. *In the Middle: Writing, Reading, and Learning with Adolescents*. Portsmouth, NH: Boynton/Cook.

Boomer, Garth. 1992. "Negotiating the Curriculum." In Garth Boomer, Nancy Lester, Cynthia Onore, and Jon Cook, eds. *Negotiating the Curriculum: Educating for the 21st Century*. London: Falmer Press.

Boomer, Garth, Nancy Lester, Cynthia Onore, and Jon Cook. 1992. *Negotiating the Curriculum: Educating for the 21st Century*. London: Falmer Press.

Fisher Bobbi. 1991. *Joyful Learning: A Whole Language Kindergarten*. Portsmouth, NH: Heinemann.

Graves, Donald. 1989. *Investigate Nonfiction*. Portsmouth, NH: Heinemann.

Jorgensen, Karen. 1993. *History Workshop: Reconstructing the Past with Elementary Students*. Portsmouth, NH: Heinemann.

Patterson, Katherine. 1991. *Lyddie*. New York: Trumpet Club.

Reid, Jo-Anne, Peter Forrestal and Johnathan Cook. 1989. *Small Group Learning in the Classroom*. Portsmouth, NH: Heinemann.

Rief, Linda. 1992. *Seeking Diversity: Language Arts with Adolescents*. Portsmouth, NH: Heinemann.

Tate, Eleanor. 1987. *The Secret of Gumbo Grove*. New York: Bantam.

Tunnell, Michael, and Richard Ammon. 1993. *The Story of Ourselves: Teaching History Through Children's Literature*. Portsmouth, NH: Heinemann.

Vygotsky, Lev. 1978. *Mind in Society: The Development of Higher Psychological Processes*. Cambridge, MA: Harvard University Press.

Contributors

Judy Blatt teaches third grade at the Haynes School in Sudbury, Massachusetts. She has always had a strong interest in bringing drama into the classroom and gives workshops for teachers interested in sharing simulations with their students.

Bill Brummett has recently decided to go back to school after twenty-seven years of public school teaching. He is now a full-time doctoral student in the field of whole language at Indiana University, studying with Jerry Harste and Carolyn Burke.

Carli Carrara teaches third grade at the Henry Barnard Laboratory School at Rhode Island College in Providence, Rhode Island, where she is an Assistant Professor. Carli shares workshops with teachers interested in integrated learning in the classroom.

Pat Cordeiro is Associate Professor in Elementary Education at Rhode Island College. Previously, she taught elementary school for eighteen years. Her present concern is the advancement and promotion of classroom teachers.

Bobbi Fisher is on leave from teaching first grade at the Haynes School in Sudbury, Massachusetts. She is a writer, a teacher-researcher, and an educational consultant. She recently was featured in a video entitled "Classroom Close-Ups: Bobbi Fisher: Organization and Management."

Lisa Burley Maras teaches an intermediate multi-age class in Genesco, New York. She recently published two chapters in *Basal Readers: A Second Look*, edited by Patrick Shannon and Ken Goodman.

Jane Rowe teaches fifth grade and is an educational consultant. She has a strong interest in critical thinking and integrated curriculum development. Jane has received a number of teaching awards, including the Kohl International Teaching Award in 1989.

Linda Squire teaches pre-kindergarten- through twelfth-grade music, both general and choral. She is interested in developing integrated curriculum at all levels and believes that music belongs across the curriculum. Her current planning work is with a junior high geography teacher.

Sandra Wilensky is Staff Leader/Principal at the F. A. Merriam School in Acton, Massachusetts. She is an experienced teacher of pre-school through fifth-grade students, and has a strong interest in developing curriculum.